BROADSTAIRS & ST PETERS DURING THE GREAT WAR OF 1914 – 1918

BROADSTAIRS & ST PETERS DURING THE GREAT WAR OF 1914 – 1918

Compiled by
Tony Euden

Published by
Michaels Bookshop
Ramsgate 2006

First published
By
Michaels Bookshop
© Tony Euden

ISBN13: 978-1905477-807
ISBN 1-905477-80-5

BROADSTAIRS & ST PETERS DURING THE GREAT WAR OF 1914 – 1918

Most of the following reports have been culled from the local newspapers of the time, chiefly the *Broadstairs & St Peters Mail*, which incorporated *The Thanet News* & *The East Kent Times*. This had its offices at the hub of the town at the Broadway. The intention is give a flavour of what the town was like during this period. It is not intended to be a record of those who served, or their records of service, but of what happened in the town & to those who were left behind.

Broadstairs, like most of the country, was completely unaware of the impending war throughout the first part of 1914. Being a town reliant on visitors, & therefore its seaside attractions, it battled on, but as numbers of men left the town for service, from the August Bank Holiday onwards, a form of paralysis set in, & everything slowed down to an unprecedented level. The Council tried its best to struggle on as normal, mostly succeeding, as something between 600 & 700 men left the town, with approximately 160 never to return. Everything was run on a shoestring, from the gas works in Albion Street, to the tramway system. The Council gradually became depleted of workers, & the shops became empty of managers & counter hands. Food became scarce & as horses became requisitioned, trade deliveries came almost to a standstill.

It was a great opportunity for the women left behind to take on the men's jobs. Firstly they appeared in the shops as counter assistants, then at the railway station & Post Office. They were taken on as conductresses on the trams, but never as drivers. Apart from working, most of their spare time was spent knitting, doing charity work or raising funds for the soldiers & sailors. Bottles & newspapers were collected for recycling for war charities. There were some paid domestic duties at the few hotels & boarding houses which managed to keep going.

A major success, which received more praise in the press than anything else was *"The Little League of Helpers"*, as it got dubbed by the *"Mail"*, a name that stuck throughout the war, a Broadstairs first, which other towns copied. The *"Little League"* was the main source of parcels to Broadstairs & St Peters serving men, & the Prisoners of War scattered around Germany.

Troops were billeted in the town in the various lodging establishments, but there were never enough troops to fill all the beds available. French & Belgian refugees were soon followed by wounded servicemen in 1914, & *"Fairfield"*, *"Roseneath"*, & the *"Yarrow"* Hospitals were quickly set up.

Throughout the war, there were restrictions on what could & couldn't be printed in the local press. Anything that could be used by the Germans as propaganda was strictly off limits, & for this reason, bombing raids & bomb damage were only reported in general terms, actual locations weren't given until the war was over.

Dr Brightman, the Council Chairman, tried on many occasions to put a Roll of Honour together, of all the Broadstairs & St Peters serving men, but was unsuccessful for many reasons.

BROADSTAIRS, ST PETERS & THE GREAT WAR

1914

On 21st January 1914, probably the first local intimation of war was at a Reservist's Concert held at The Grand Pavilion in Westcliff Road. *The event was to raise £250 for a rifle range in Broadstairs to be used by the 28th (Broadstairs) Company of the Kent National Reserve, the Territorials & the Boy Scouts for rifle practice. Captain Peyton R N, the Officer Commanding of the 28th (Broadstairs) Company said, "If all those present read the daily papers, they would see month by month, year by year, that the war clouds were gathering over Europe, & it behove every able bodied man to prepare for the time when he would be called upon to defend his country, his own hearth & home". The 28th already had 97 men on the roll, but they were no good unless they knew how to use arms. Their desire was to build the rifle range at Broadstairs, & he could see no problems with a town like Broadstairs being able to raise such funds. The outstanding feature of the second position of the programme was a tableau, which consisted of all the artistes who had taken part in the evening's entertainment. It was entitled, "Past, Present & Future", which gave a vivid picture of Britain's fighting men. In the centre of the company were John Bull, & the figure of Britannia. Veterans, with their long rows of medals, The Buffs Cyclists, & sailors with fixed bayonets surrounded them. Accompanying them were the Boy Scouts, & members of the local fire brigade. Whilst they all stood, John Bull gave a fine rendering of Rule Britannia, all good rousing patriotic stuff.*

Broadstairs & St Peters Mail 21stJan 1914

The national newspapers may have been full of the impending war, but Broadstairs continued as usual. In July the 3rd Kings Own Hussars were playing at the bandstand, & the town was arguing over whether 16/- a week was enough wage for the newly appointed Pierremont Gardens caretaker. He said he was quite happy with it, but others thought differently. The clock chimes at St Peters church had stopped ringing at the request of Colonel Prideaux of "Hopeville", on account of his invalid wife not being able to sleep. The village took umbrage & a petition was raised to confront the vicar. It was a hot summer, holidaymakers still flocked to the town, & the bathing machines, & seaside concessions were still doing well. *An added attraction was the 1st Battle Squadron anchored in the Downs on the 8th July. The eight vessels, all dreadnoughts, made a fine sight as they came up, & anchored in two rows off Deal.* Two days later, the 5th Battle Squadron, all of the "King Edward" class were spotted off the Foreland. Local boats reaped a rich harvest taking visitors out to see the ships. On July 15th, Broadstairs had the opportunity of seeing eight water planes in full flight as they passed over the town at high speed.

The annual swim from the Ramsgate Iron Pier to Broadstairs Harbour took place last Saturday, & was won by Mr Boucher of Broadstairs, who completed the 2 & a half-mile swim in 60 minutes, wrote the Mail. The only militants in the town were the Suffragettes, who had kept their heads down since the shenanigans at Margate. On 29th July, The Kent Cyclists Battalion were at camp at Callis Court, the home of Mr H H Marks. Twenty officers & 450 men were in attendance for the fortnight, & were receiving instruction, *"in the work they would have to undertake in time of war"*.

By the 5th August, the mood of the country started to change. Refugees started to arrive from the continent into the Thanet towns.

The B & St P Mail reported

"It is difficult to find the words to adequately express our feelings at the great war Germany has plunged us into. In fact the time for words has gone by, but deep in the heart of every Englishman is a great wrath at the Kaiser's mad folly in plunging the whole of Europe into a war. We know the zeal that men of our Army & Navy & Territorial Forces have responded to the call of duty; it now remains for those of us who are non-combatants to do out part. We should be prepared, as civilians, to do whatever work lies in our power to back up those who have the destiny of this nation in their hands'"

A fleet of taxis & charabancs were requested to arrive at Callis Court at 8 am on the 5th. The Officers of the Kent Cycle Battalion commandeered the lot, *"Relinquishing the chauffeurs of their charges"*. Returning visitors were also put out when they found the army had commandeered the local train service.

Of the hundreds of French & Belgian schoolchildren receiving their education in Thanet, the youths were called back to their countries for mobilisation. In connection with mobilisation, a number of Austrian

& German chefs & waiters, engaged at the various hotels & cafes in the district, were entrained to London, en-route to their own countries.

Posted in prominent areas of the town were the notices

MOBILISATION ORDER
ARMY RESERVE, REGULAR, SPECIAL RESERVE

HIS MAJESTY THE KING HAS BEEN GRACIOUSLY PLEASED TO DIRECT BY PROCLAMATION THAT THE ARMY RESERVE BE CALLED OUT ON PERMANENT SERVICE.
All Regular Reservists are required to report themselves, **AT ONCE**, to their place of joining in accordance with the instructions on their identity certificates for the purpose of joining the Army.

CARE OF THE SICK & WOUNDED
The following appeal has been issued by the Officers commanding of the Kent Voluntary Aid Detachment, (VAD) of the Territorial Force.
An order having been received for the above attachment to be ready for DUTY. Anyone willing to help by personal service, money, stores or material, is asked to apply to the Headquarters Drill Hall, Wilsons Road, Ramsgate. Help is urgently needed with this appeal.

The Rush for Provisions.
The Mail reported, "*This began on Saturday. Some of the local grocers had orders out of all proportions to the needs of their customers. Many well-to-do people, who could afford to stand the burden of higher prices, were lying in of stocks for weeks to come. This indiscriminate buying must bear more hardly on the poor. Prices are advancing, but the rush that is now taking place will only force the prices up higher. Many of the shops in the town had to shut early yesterday, so that they can complete their orders. Other shops shut early, because they had run out of produce to complete any orders*".

Four days after the outbreak of war, on the 8th August 1914, Broadstairs & St Peters Council set up an Emergency Committee to deal with the crises. The nucleus was formed around the Councillors with 18 co-opted people from around the town. All doctors, ministers occupying pulpits in the town, the secretary of the United Benefit Service & the secretary of the Soldiers & Sailors Families Association, were all invited, The Urban district Council, & the Poor Law Guardians were asked to send representatives. Five lady members, with experience in relief work, were also on the committee. The work before the committee was

A, Collection fund to be shared to other public funds as they thought expedient.
B, Collection of gifts in kind to benefit the sick & wounded.
C, Control of sale of foodstuffs & to prevent hoarding by individuals
D, Adoption of a means to allay panic & to offer advice & assistance where necessary.

Mr. W Blackburn, of York Street, immediately stepped in & offered his warehouse, plus a man & horse & cart, all free of charge. Within the month £388 had been distributed, & Mr. Blackburn's store held 15 bolsters, 22 blankets, & 47 sheets, all gratefully received.
Fifty more Broadstairs men were sworn in as special constables during September. Mr A Olby, the owner of the Vale Estates, & Mr H H Marks of Callis Court offered recently cultivated land for use as allotments, for the duration. The Mail reported, "*It is no use waiting until the hard times are upon us. A little hard work now will bring rewards in the winter months. This is not a charity scheme, its value lies in*

preserving the self reliant spirit of our race, & a manly spirit, which will be required to the utmost in the months, or perhaps even years to come". The fifty plots in the Vale & twenty eight plots at Grange Road were all quickly taken, Councilor Foster being the organizer.

A month later, Kent County Council suggested that councils throughout Kent, should set up Emergency Committees for relief work, Broadstairs Council just sent the message back,

"Done".

On the 12th August the Mail reported

Owing to War Office orders, all of the military bands, which were to fulfil their engagements during the holidays, were withdrawn. The Council Band Committee has shown ready recourse to fill the gap & have engaged a string band, The Bijou Orchestra, to play at the Bandstand over the next few weekends. It is next to impossible to secure a full instrumental band. The Bohemia was full to capacity. Right from the opening chorus, "Gay Bohemians are We", the company enter into the zest for their work.

During the same week, *"a large number of men left the town to take part in the war. Several ex-servicemen have volunteered for work of one kind or another, throughout, a number of cyclists & motorcyclists in khaki have been buzzing in & around Broadstairs, sometimes in groups & sometimes singly".*

The first of the local men to enlist after the outbreak of war had been declared in August, were the Reserves & the Territorial Regiments. These were quickly moved away, & were re-introduced to the skills they had known on previous active service. They were quickly formed into the Expeditionary Forces, & sent to France or Belgium & into the thick of the action.

A second army was soon required by Lord Kitchener, & volunteers were quickly called for. These volunteers would be untrained raw recruits, & local companies were quickly formed. Broadstairs, like the other two towns, had its own Volunteer Reserve, & had little kit & no uniforms, the only outward sign being a Khaki arm band surmounted by a crown. At first recruiting was slow with only ten volunteers in the first week; however with the formation of groups within the volunteers the numbers increased. The idea was for like minded groups of people to enlist together, this enabled men who worked together to stay together, but also enabled you to keep your social standing in the town, whatever that was, intact, so traders stayed with traders & bank managers stayed with their own kind, the professional classes, such was the class divide in 1914.

Basic training was expected to take around seven weeks, but with so little kit to be trained with, the Volunteers were put to good use, guarding "things", route marching, & coastal watching. Weekends were spent, combined with Ramsgate & Margate's Volunteers, in camp often at Cliffsend, Wingham, or Canterbury, usually having to route march to the site. Church parades were always another good excuse to combine the three groups together in a route march to Westgate or Birchington.

Once in the Volunteers, the recruiting sergeants made their regular visits, & the fittest men, between the ages of nineteen & thirty eight were creamed off. Later this was reduced to eighteen, though it was still not permitted to have Volunteers on the Front till they were nineteen. At first as a Volunteer, men were able to designate which regiment they wanted to join. The recruiting sergeants did their best to spread the influx of volunteers around, but most men held out for their regiment of choice. Skilled mechanics were picked off quickly for the Royal Engineers, drivers for the Ambulance Corps, though most ambulances were still horse driven.

As more men enlisted & left the town, even the local scout troop were called into action. The Mail reported

The Scouts Work, Efficiency of the Broadstairs Troops.

As conclusive proof of the excellent work performed by the Boy Scouts, the Government have now recognised their uniform as the uniform of a Public Service non-military body. On Saturday, a detachment were on duty near to the Power House, (Northdown Road), when some sparks from an engine set on fire several sheaves of corn. When the Scouts got to work, there were 40 sheaves alight, but labouring with skill & energy, gained the upper hand. The Scouts have pitched camp near to the Railway Station, & have the duties of patrolling all of the prominent buildings of the town. *They are also guarding the pump house at Rumfields, & keeping watch on the coast at nights.*

The Mail started to publish the names of all the enlisted men & volunteers. Of the 107 from Broadstairs & St Peters, 85 were in the National Reserve, 8 in the 4th Battalion of the Buffs, 2 joined the Surrey Yeomanry, 4 were in the Kent Cyclist Battalion, & 8 were in the Local Guard of Volunteers. The Local Guard were all over age to transfer to the regular forces.

One week later on August 19th, there was a recruiting rally at the bandstand, where the Council Chairman, Dr Brightman, spoke to a large crowd about patriotism, duty, & the call to the flag. *"The country was after time expired men, (veterans), up to the age of 42, & new recruits between the ages of 19 & 30. Let them come forward, many have responded. If Lord Kitchener does not get the men for whom he asks, an Act in the nature of the Military Act can be passed through Parliament in less than a day".* Thirteen new recruits came forward & signed up.

On the civilian front nursing & first aid lectures were held by Dr Robins at the Metropolitan Homes in Lanthorne Road. Many Broadstairs ladies were assisting with the fitting out of Chatham House School in Ramsgate as an emergency hospital. Working parties were set up, knitting gloves, underwear, & bonnets for the troops, previously unheard of in August. The Yarrow Convalescent Home tried to scotch rumours that it was being converted into a Military Hospital, a rumour that became a fact within two months. Clothing was being supplied to the needy who had lost their breadwinner by the Prince of Wales Relief Fund.

Broadstairs Council were still re-iterating that the town, though close to the continent, was not at any risk, & there was no reason why visitors should not visit. Alarmists & scaremongers were rife in the rest of the country, but Broadstairs remained unscathed by the rumours that it was amongst the first to be shelled, & it was full of spies

The Mail reported

"Though it by no means presents the usual spectacle of thronging crowds, the scene on Broadstairs Front is not greatly different from that which we see in ordinary times. The beach & esplanades are still crowded. The entertainments are still well patronised, & the town is still essentially a pleasure resort".

On the other front, most of the Broadstairs veterans & reservists reported to Chatham House School or Wilsons Hall in Ramsgate, Chatham House for the East Kent Battery of the Royal Field Artillery, or Wilsons Hall for the East Kent Buffs.

Those from Chatham House received their orders to depart for Dover. *They all formed up in the school grounds, & were addressed by the Ramsgate Mayor, Councillor G Cook. In a few eloquent sentences, he commended the men on their patriotism, & wished them all God speed. His words were received with resounding cheers, which was taken up by the huge crowd of citizens outside the gates. The attachment of over 200 men, moved into the roadway in four columns, & proceeded to march down Chatham Street, the High Street, & Queen Street, which presented a remarkable scene, as headed by their officers they marched through the town on the commencement of their 18 mile tramp to Dover.*

Every vantage point was occupied by men women & children all eager to catch a glimpse, & all along the route there rang from every throat cheer, after cheer, after cheer, whilst flags & sticks were waived in the air.

Those from Wilsons Hall were more fortunate, as the 100 men marched singing to the station to catch a train to Dover.

Appeals for accommodation for French & Belgian refugees were issued by the various churches in Broadstairs, which were readily taken up as the visitors started to leave the town. Some troops remained in the town, & charity football matches were set up at Lindenthorpe playing fields for the Belgian Relief Fund. Such teams as the "Mowhawks", the "Broadstairs Bloods", "Kentish Cobbs" & "Goorkhas" were quickly formed amongst the soldiers.

The Army Travelling Bureau was back in the town on the 16th September at the Rose Inn Yard. *A detachment of the 4th Battalion of the Buffs was accompanied by the Yantians Band who struck up rousing tunes.* The Chairman Mr C S Reed opened the speeches explaining why the Government wanted 100,000 men by Christmas, & every able bodied man who could be spared was wanted at the Front. At the conclusion of Captain Baird's speech requesting volunteers, the crowd cheered & clapped as a young strapping fellow stepped to the front to do his duty. At the conclusion of the meeting, the National Anthem was sung by all present. Over the next week a further 60 Broadstairs & St Peters men also stepped forward.

On September 23rd, the Council lent on the local Justices of the Peace, who issued an order to all licensed premises in Broadstairs & St Peters, that they were to be shut, & empty by 9pm each evening. This brought a near riot in the town, as it was still possible to obtain "liquid refreshments" in the other two towns till 11pm during the week. The Justices relented, & granted a temporary extension till 10pm during the week, but shortly all towns fell into line, much against the Licensed Victuallers wishes.

On September 30th, the Council received a communication from the Officer Commanding the Kent Infantry Brigade. "*In the interest of public safety, I would ask you to arrange for the use of electric street lamps to be <u>discontinued</u>, & the streets to be lighted by gas lamps only, keeping the numbers to the bare minimum*". Another communication a week later requested that all premises facing the sea, refrain from showing any lights towards the sea, by either using blinds or darkened lamps, (whatever they were). Any street lighting on promenades or seafront roads was to be kept to a minimum, & those left on were to be painted a dark colour on the skyward & seaward sides. Once again protests were put to the Council, but this time it was Government Orders.

Also on the 30th September, "*the kindness of Mr O W Marsh in allowing the Territorials in Broadstairs to bathe absolutely free of charge, has been appreciated & they will regret to see the last bathing machine leave the beach this week. The bathe of about 60 men every morning has aroused considerable interest in the town*"

. That same week, the first of the local casualties were reported.

BROADSTAIRS MEN ON SUNKEN CRUISERS Sep 30th
Cressy Man Returns

Five Broadstairs men, so far as we can gather, were on the doomed cruisers, which sank in the North Sea. They are R H Brenchley, J F Horn, E A Jordan &, T J Miller, all of H M S Cressy, A V Strong of H M S Akoubir. Of these only one name has appeared on the lists of those saved, & that is E A Jordon. Of the rest nothing has been heard.

E A Jordan is now on leave & is staying at Reading Street. Jordan had the good fortune to be on one of the lifeboats & was saved. Before the occurrence of the sinking of the cruisers he wrote to his fiancee very cheerfully saying that he was in the best of health & high spirits.

Another man is Able Seaman Gunner Albert V Strong of H M S Akoubir. Albert Strong will probably be best known as one of the finest swimmers Broadstairs has ever seen, & has over & over saved many lives. The last occasion was at Broadstairs when he assisted in the rescue of a drowning man off the pier. Most of his other feats have been carried out in foreign waters. When he joined the Navy & his ability was

T J Miller   Albert Strong   J F Horne   Robert Brenchley

recognised, he was entrusted with the teaching of the Navy boys to swim. Strong was down at Broadstairs a week or so ago when the Cressy put into Chatham. In his short notes to his mother he assured her he was in good spirits, & was confident that they would be able to thrash the enemy.

Blacksmith Robert Henry Brenchley of Albion Street, was also serving on H M S Cressy, & belonged to Chatham Naval Reserve, having spent 22 years in the Royal Navy. He was a native of Broadstairs & the proud owner of a Good Conduct Medal. He has been employed at the Broadstairs Cinema since its opening in 1912, & was only called up to re-join on August Bank Holiday. Up to the present Mrs Brenchley has heard nothing as to his fate.

Two other men with homes in Reading Street were on the ill-fated H M S Cressy. They are 1st Class P O J F Horn, & 1st Class Stoker T J Miller. Of neither has anything been heard. We understand that P O Horn was working on the gun that fired at the enemy's submarines.

Others were more fortunate, as is the case of Private Whitehead of the 2nd Battalion of the West Riding Regiment, whose home was at 5 Napier Road St Peters

GREAT RETREAT FROM MONS

With a sun-tanned face due to exposure in all weathers, Private Whitehead is at home for a few days recuperating.

Called at the declaration of hostilities he says, *"We landed at Havre in France on 16th August & marched to base camp. The following morning we went to the station & travelled for 20 hours to Moirelles. We then marched for 22 miles to the Belgian border at Revael, which we reached on the 21st. We then proceeded to Mons where we divided into billets. On Sunday 23 August, the first shot was fired by the Germans, & just as we were about to have dinner, we were given the order, "Prepare for action". We were watching shots raining over the houses near to where we were waiting. On the Sunday night we were given orders to retire, & we spent all night marching to Hornu, where we took up fresh positions. At Hornu we*

Private Whitehead

were surrounded on three sides by the Germans, & we gave then all our worth, & whilst our losses were light, the Germans were brought down like corn in front of a reapers scythe. Although our men put up vigorous resistance we were forced to retire down the street behind us. I had a narrow escape when a shot dropped in the road, hitting the heel plate of my boot.

When we reached the bridge further down the road, volunteers were called for to line the bridge whilst all the men retreated, & I amongst others stepped forward. We held the bridge for the next two hours till all the men were over, & I lost my company & so joined the 14th Brigade.

During the battle of Mons, the officers distinguished themselves. The German losses were considerably more than the Allies, & the conduct of the men in the trenches was excellent. From Mons we retired to Swasts near to the French border, & then proceeded another 23 miles from Mons, where we were able to re-join our own brigade. About three the next morning we marched to Cambrai & we took up position with the Dorsets in their trenches. We were under fire from 6 in the morning till 4.30 that afternoon. General Ferguson asked for volunteers to make the last stand to enable the men in the trenches to recoup. From there we proceeded to St Quintain where we had a rest & a great breakfast. We were informed that the Germans were not far behind, & so decamped, & marched another 18 miles over the Thursday & Friday to Joulsey & Creppy. The Germans were still close on the Monday morning, so we opened fire on them. A whole Corps of Germans were completely cut off, & returned the fire. After the order to retire, we took two cars, 6 officers, some Privates & 2 machine guns to Montreul.

All through these engagements we were exposed to all weathers, often lying in wet trenches & choked with the smoke from the guns. I was sick with the fever & ague, & was conveyed by field ambulance to the base at Mons. I was transferred to Lemons, & on to St Nazaire, & then home.

I will be leaving Broadstairs on Saturday & return to Halifax, & then back to the front." His opinion of the German artillery was that they are well trained, but weak in infantry. Most of the German prisoners were quite happy & declined to return home. The Belgian women were wonderful, & would give almost anything they thought would be useful to the troops. When the troops passed through the streets of Belgium, women & children lined the streets, anxious to shake the hands of the soldiers. They provided them with water by leaving buckets by the side of the roads with two or three glasses close by.

Concluding Private Whitehead said *"most of the men were quite happy & whilst waiting in the trenches, they were always singing familiar songs"*.

14th October 1914

(Private Whitehead was given a medical discharge on arriving at Halifax, & sent home.)

FAIRFIELD HOUSE IS A HOSPITAL. Mr Craig's Generosity

Mr Norman Craig, Member of Parliament for Thanet, has not only gone into the most dangerous of branches of the Navy, but has lent his handsome residence for the duration. Fairfield House is being converted into a hospital for wounded soldiers. Its spacious apartments have been converted into wards & sick rooms. Nearly every room has been given up to this purpose, & 30 to 40 patients will be taken in. Mr Craig's office is the doctors room & the large dining room is the nurses common room. There is also plenty of room for resident nurses & others. The ladies of the town have converted the house, & there is nothing ostentatious in the work, nothing remarkable or likely to attract attention, & evoke praise to the casual observer.

Dr Frank Brightman & Dr Robins are the Medical Officers, Mrs F Brightman the Commandant, Mrs Minns the trained head nurse, & Miss Marks the Quarter master. There is a staff of about 30. Eleven Belgian wounded arrived last Wednesday & another 15 are expected to arrive from Ramsgate today.

BELGIAN REFUGEES

With the influx of Belgian refugees into this country, Broadstairs has received its liberal share. Everywhere one goes in the town one sees people wearing a little ribbon of black, orange & red. By the kindness of the people of the Whittuck Home on the East Cliff, 4 destitute Belgian women & 14 children have been made at home. It is now feared that they will all be moved out of Broadstairs as it is in the restricted area for foreigners. It is expected that Belgian wounded will use the Whittuck Home.

About eighty men of the 2nd Home Counties Field Ambulance were billeted in St Peters last week. The Officers are accommodated in the vicarage, which will also be used as the orderly room.

There was a parade of Special Constables at the Grand Pavilion last week, where Mr E S Oak-Rhind, their Chief, reminded the men of their duties, & the penalties if they failed.

Dr Kelly Patterson has offered his seaside residence, Bleak House, to be used as a convalescent home for wounded soldiers. This was turned down as being unsuitable.

The teachers & the staff of the St Peters Schools have turned the parish room into a reading room for the troops. Books & games have been plentifully supplied through the united efforts of Mrs Hare & Mrs Taylor the schools head teachers.

Probably not knowing was the hardest part, amongst many of the letters home was one in the Mail on November 4th.

CAPTURED BY THE GERMANS

Mrs Wish of Edge End Road has received a letter from her son E J Wish R N V R, who is a prisoner of the Germans. Writing from Dobritz, he says, *"I have had a most exciting experience this week. We were in the trenches at Antwerp for 3 days, but had to withdraw, so effective was the shellfire against our little rifles. I have managed to escape death time after time & have seen many good fellows killed next to me. Whilst retiring to another position, we were on a refugee train & were surrounded. Part of the train was wrecked, & we were rounded up & taken prisoner. We are now in a camp in Dobritz. I will not be allowed to write again as we all have to take it in turn".*

There were now 69 Belgian wounded soldiers under the V A D at Fairfield, the Whittuck or Roseneath. The wants of the hospital are gifts of large bath towels & gramophone needles. Wounded British soldiers were beginning to arrive, & these were ferried from the station to the Yarrow Home by Field Ambulances. The first 79 arrived from Dover on November 18th.

December 2nd.

The girls of St Peters School are all working with zeal making various garments for the Defenders of the Empire during the winter months. One class of girls subscribes to the cost of the postage, whereas the whole school unites & contributes to the materials. So far 28 parcels have been sent to headquarters, & consist of gloves, mittens, body belts, & chest protectors. The recipients of the parcels have written back to the pupils.

1st Class Stoker Harry Shersby of H M S Russell writes, "The parcel arrived safely, & is much appreciated. There is only one thing the sailors are grumbling about, & that is that the Germans are staying in harbour. I wish they would only come out & fight".

James Carter R N sends his thanks, "the woollen articles will be useful now that winter is here in the North Sea. We often long for a roaring fire & a comfortable chair, but up to the present we'll only be getting the roaring fire of the enemy's guns, that's if they ever come out".

In is interesting to note that over 150 boys who have been educated at St Peters Boys School, are now serving with various branches of H M forces. A Roll of Honour is being prepared & framed by the present scholars. & will hang in a prominent position in the school.

Besides the worsening weather at the Front, some troops were still in good humour.

Writing to his wife, Lance Corporal Robert Stead of the 1st Battalion of the Buffs says, "I have a bit of a cold at present, & to make it worse a wretched German has torn a hole in my overcoat with one of his bullets. It is the one thing we all depend on now to keep us warm. At night another bullet entered my valise, making a hole in my mess tin, & spoiling my notepaper & envelopes. I found the bullet in my biscuits. I should like to get hold of the bounder who sent it".

To his sister he wrote, "We are having a splendid time up here picnicking in the trenches. We get plenty to eat & a fireworks display every night. The Germans generally give us a hot breakfast with their guns & keep it up all day, & half the night, we get a little of our back now & again. I am in good spirits & living well. We eat our bully beef & jam & throw the tins at the Germans to put their sausages in. One thing we get out of out here is the washing up the cups & saucers".

IMPRISONED BY THE GERMANS ……….30th December 1914

Broadstairs & St Peters Mail

Nurses Graphic Revelations of German Hatred.

Nurse Bowie is the eldest daughter of Councillor Bowie of Elmwood Farm Broadstairs, & went to the front in the early days of the war. She said that after embarking from Folkestone on August 15th, & with other nurses of Lady Manners party of Nurses & a doctor, they proceeded to Brussels via Ostend. When they reached Brussels, Nurse Bowie said the Belgians & Red Cross met them with enthusiasm, & a convent was soon converted into a hospital with all the necessary equipment. A week later they were treating six Belgian soldiers when the German Army marched into Brussels. All the Belgian wounded were taken away as prisoners of war. After a few days some wounded German soldiers were brought into the hospital. It was not till then that Nurse Bowie heard that the English were at Mons. They were ordered by the German Officials to move out, & moved to a large Belgian townhouse on the outskirts of the city. The Belgians once again helped to fit the house out. On 30th of August the Germans brought in British wounded, & the next night some prisoners of war were brought into the town.

Nurse BOWIE, with the Red Cross Nurses on Foreign Service.

They had to accommodate them all. By this time over seventy beds were occupied. The Germans started to become very spiteful, particularly the Officers. They were continuously kept under surveillance & were not allowed to move around without permission. The nurses then approached the American Ambassador, to try & get their passports back so they could leave. The Germans in Brussels relented, returned their passports & sent them to Mons, under escort.

Going to the Hotel de Ville in Mons, they were told by the German Officers that they could go no further, & refused any more help. They were threatened with arrest when they announced that they wanted to return to England. The German hate for the English was growing very intense, & the party were finally arrested & taken back to the Hotel de Ville. Notwithstanding the pouring rain, the Germans marched them to Mauberg, & instead of granting them their release, they were thrown into prison, & they were given no food whatsoever. About 6.30 next morning the German guards brought round half a stale loaf, which they poked through a grating in the door. Nurse Bowie smiled as she said, " we kept warm by putting a bed in the middle of the cell & marched round it singing". Because they made so much noise singing & talking, the German guards moved them to a more secluded room. Diner was served at 11.30 & was a watery, greasy stuff that was totally inedible. About 6 o'clock the Belgian authorities from Mons demanded an interview with the nurses & after that, conditions started to improve, including the conduct of the Germans towards them.

Whenever they were required at the hospital, German guards with rifles & fixed bayonets escorted them. After being confined for five days, they were released, & left prison around mid-day on the 4th December. A senior German Commander in Brussels had signed their papers, but on leaving they were re-arrested & taken under escort by three German guards to Aix La Chapelle. The German Officers were very bitter towards them, & they were mocked sneeringly, saying that they would soon be in Paris, & London was only a minute away. In the drenching rain they were marched to the army barracks & were finally given permission to leave the country by way of Cologne, Osnabruche & Hamburg.

From Hamburg they went to Vandru in Denmark, where they found the Danes very helpful & sympathetic. From Vandru they went to Copenhagen & on to Bergen, & crossed the North Sea in a Norwegian trading vessel. On the 17th December they went down the east Scottish coast & landed at Newcastle.

Nurse Bowie said one of the reasons they were imprisoned by the Germans, was they said that the English had done the same. They said that they didn't bother about the Belgians & the French. They could put up with them, but the English were "Perfect Devils" because they would do anything.

Nurse Bowie said that in spite of all she has had to put up with under the Germans, she would go back to the front & attend our wounded soldiers.

Meanwhile back in Broadstairs

TROOPS FOR BROADSTAIRS
Petition Sent to War Office

The stress of war is beginning to be felt in Broadstairs & it is feared that householders whose income from letting during the past season has been seriously effected, & could be faced with a harsh winter.

With a view of reducing the possibility of such a state of affairs, a number of householders & tradesmen have signed a petition, asking the War Office to billet troops in the town, which will materially benefit both tradesmen & householders. The petition, which has over 200 signatures, was sent to the War Office last Sunday. The number of troops being asked for is 5,000. The suggestion has been in the public mind for some time now, & when it was known that the suggestion was being taken up seriously & the authorities approached on the matter, the response amongst the residents was unanimous. The petition signed by 86 tradesmen was also brought before the Council, who gave the petition their full support.

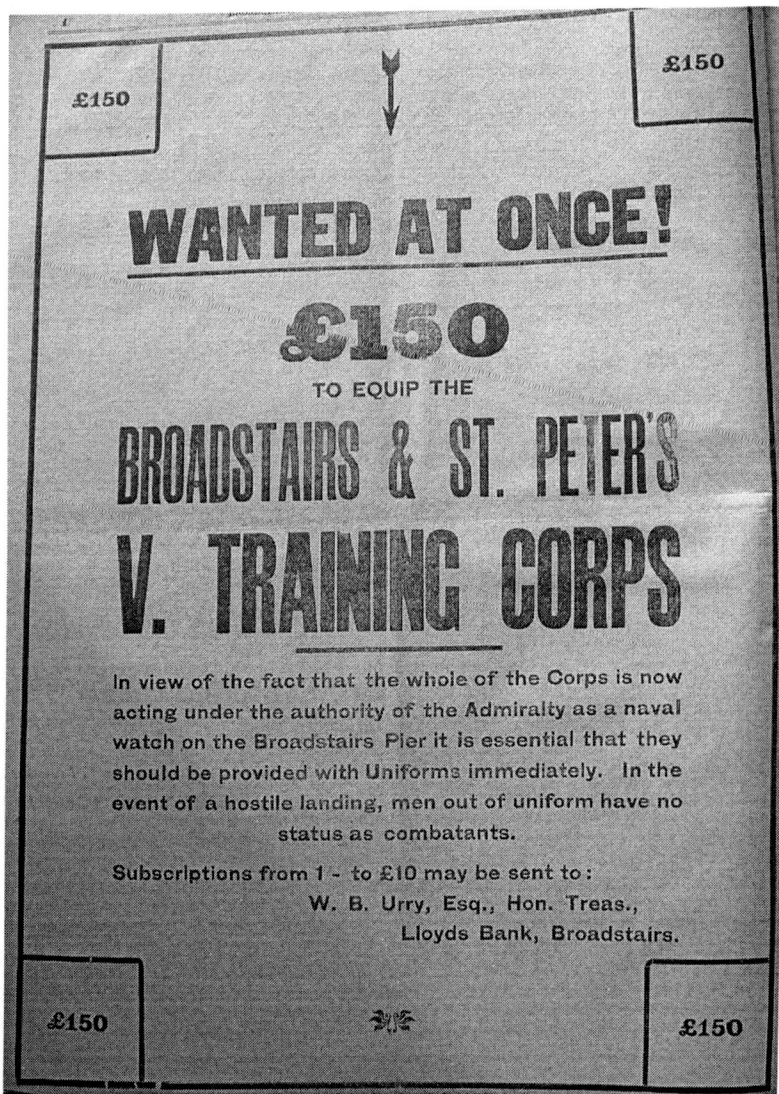

By the end of 1914, the British Expeditionary Force in Flanders was suffering from 90% casualties. They had met the Germans at Mons, but had been forced to retreat 170 miles, fighting all the way. They had chased the enemy across the Rivers Marne & Aisne, & held them up at a town called Ypres. Now it was the time for the Territorials & Volunteers to reinforce the lines, & become soldiers under the hardest of situations.

THE ANGEL OF MONS Sept 1914

Since the first major battle of the war at Mons in August & September 1914, many troops who returned home either wounded, or for a rest, had stories of their experiences to tell to others. One of the many stories concerned the story of guardian angels, convincing them & other fighting soldiers that what they were doing was in the right. To those reluctant volunteers for the front, these stories were use to persuade them that everything would be OK as they had a guardian angel to protect them, after all the soldiers had seen them. The Church was very quick to latch on to the idea of guardian angels, whilst the sceptics were very quick to discount the idea as an illusion of confused minds. The debate was used from many pulpits to convince sceptics, Broadstairs pulpits being no different to others.

HEAVENLY VISION - AN ANGELIC DELIVERANCE

BROADSTAIRS MINISTER ON THE ANGEL OF MONS

The much discussed topic "The Angel of Mons", was dealt with by the Rev W Muncaster, the Congregational Minister of Broadstairs, during the week.

Immense interest, observed the speaker, had been awakened by the report, that, in the retreat of the Army at Mons, many of the soldiers saw a vision of angels, & the angels were on the side fighting for us, & really prevented the annihilation of the Expeditionary Forces.

Now Mr Arthur Macken says that the whole thing was fiction, & has no foundation in fact. He declares that the rumour of "The Angels of Mons", arose in the following manner. On the last Sunday in August 1914, London was plunged into deepest gloom by the news of the awful disaster to the British Army at Mons. Sorely troubled by the terrible accident, the journalist in question made his way to church, & there the working of his imagination, which had produced in his mind, a picture of the British Army in a furnace of agony & death, began to make up a story, as he said, "While the deacon was singing the Gospels". Afterwards the plot a story occurred to him. This story entitled, "The Bowmen", was published in September. The pith of the story was that when one portion of the British Army seemed on the point of utter destruction, one of the soldiers remembered a queer vegetarian restaurant in London, where all the plates had printed on them, a figure of St George. Surrounding the figure was the motto "May St George be a present help to the English". The soldier, as he fired, uttered the motto, & then the roar of battle seemed to die down to a gentle murmur, & he heard thousands shouting, " St George, St George for merry England!" & he saw before him a long line of shapes with a shinning about them. They were like men who drew the bow, & their cloud of arrows flew, singing in the air towards the German hosts. The issue was that 10.000 German soldiers lay dead before that little company, & the mysterious part was that no wounds were discernible on the bodies of the dead German soldiers.

The Rev Muncaster said that if we observe that this story was fiction, & the writer says that the account of the angels at Mons have had their origin in that, was the story true? Was there no such vision of angels as has been rumoured? Is it all moonshine, this talk of a marvellous interposition of shinning ones? It was all a question of evidence. Was it possible to produce a man, who, at the Battle of Mons, saw a vision of angels with his own eyes? Lying in an English hospital, there is a wounded soldier who has made a definite statement with regard to this matter. He says that he was with his battalion at the retreat at Mons, on the 29th August, between 8 & 9 o'clock in the evening, & he was standing with nine other men on duty, when an officer suddenly came up in a state of great agitation & asked them if they ha d seen anything astonishing. He then went on to the next party on guard. Afterwards the officer came back & taking that soldier with the others a few yards away showed them the sky. Then he saw in mid air a strange light which became brighter, & revealed three shapes, one in the centre having what looked like outstretched wings, the other two were not so large, but were distinct from the centre one. They appeared to have a long loose hanging garment of a golden tint. They were above the German lines facing the English trenches. They stood watching the figures for about three-quarters of an hour. Other men came up, who stated that they had seen the same thing.

There was another account from a nurse who attended a Lancashire Fusilier. He asked for a picture or a medal of St George, because he had seen him on a white horse leading the British when the Allies turned at Mons. Another wounded man noticing the nurse's look of amazement, said to her, "Its true, sister, we all saw it. First there was a sort of yellow mist before the Germans, who came on as if a solid wall; there was no end to 'em. I just give up. No use fighting the whole German race, thinks I, it's all up with us. The next minute comes this funny cloud of light, & when it clears off there is a tall man with yellow hair & golden armour, on a white horse, holding his sword up & his mouth open as if he was saying, "Come on boys". Then the Germans turned & ran away, & with us after them".

There is another aspect of this angelic deliverance, when some times a wounded man in the field became conscious of a comrade in white coming to him with help. Dr Horton related how one of their men who had heard this story put it down to hysterical excitement. But he had an experience when his division suffered loss. He fell & tried to hide in a hollow in the ground. As he lay, not daring to lift his head, he saw one in white coming to him. He thought he must be a stretcher-bearer, but it could not be, as bullets were raining all around him. The white robed one came & bent over him. For a moment the man lost consciousness, but when he came round he was out of danger. The white figure still stood over him, looking at his hand. He said" you are wounded in the hand". The soldier said that in spite of the peril & the wound, he felt a joy he had never experienced before.

Speaking generally, many of the soldiers who had fought at Mons & Ypres were conscious of some mystery & were convinced that extraordinary things had occurred.

Did the German army, one might ask, share the experienced? A lady in Germany at the time of Mons, said there was much discussion in Berlin, because a certain regiment that had been ordered to do a certain duty failed to carry out those orders, & were censored. They declared that they did go forward, but found themselves absolutely powerless to proceed. Their horses turned round & fled like the wind. A lieutenant of the regiment who was there at the time confirmed the story.

A British officer was asked by a German prisoner captured after Mons, who was it who led them, (the English), on a great white horse? Although he was such a conspicuous figure, none of the Germans were able to hit him. It also appeared that all of the Germans killed at the time had no wounds on them. The German prisoner also related, "How could we break through your lines, when you had all those thousands of troops behind you". At the time all the British had were a thin line of two regiments, with nothing in reserve at the rear.

Many of the men fighting at Mons were aware of those heavenly visitants accompanying them in the fray, but they often spoke of the inhabitants of the spiritual world as "within the veil". If only the veil could be blown aside a little, they were convinced that they would get a glimpse of the shinning hosts.

The Rev Muncaster then said, that the soldiers were fighting for right & justice, & if there was a world of spirits, was there not the probability that the angels would do what they could to help them. This was perfectly in accord with what was written in the scriptures. In the New Testament it was written, "Are there not all ministering spirits sent forth to minister for them who shall be heirs to salvation".

Broadstairs & St Peters Mail 29th Sept 1915

IS IT TRUE?

Whilst some people accept the story as being perfectly correct, the vast majority seem to be sceptical, & this has caused much discussion of late. "Echo" readers will doubtless be divided in their opinions, & most will treat the reports as nonsense. My own opinion is that it is quite likely to be true. Because angels do not appear to us in everyday life, it does not occur to me that such a thing is possible. I see no valid reason why the vision should not be seen. If all that is contained in the Bible is considered to be fact, which is commonly accepted that it is, what is there that is so extraordinary in the appearance of angels at Mons.

Editor Broadstairs & St Peters Echo 14th August 1915

13

1915

The Broadstairs Training Corps finally achieved their request of the previous year for somewhere to practice rifle shooting when Mr Blackburn set up a miniature, (.22), rifle range in the basement of his shop in York Street in January 1915.

In the Mail on the 3rd January it was reported under the headline
JITTERY BROADSTAIRS
Considerable anxiety was felt on Friday afternoon when a very loud report was heard in the direction of the Pierremont Laundry, (Ramsgate Road). Thinking it was from a hostile aircraft many people became agitated, but were relieved to find it was only a bursting of a pipe at the laundry, which smashed one of the windows.

Letters were still arriving from the Front. One on January 6th was from Rifleman Goodey of 9 Balliol Road Reading Street explaining to his parents how his Christmas went.

Rifleman Goodey is serving with the 3rd Battalion Rifle Brigade & has been at the Front since November last year, & received his baptism of fire on November 23rd. He is formerly a scholar of St Peters School & writes home, "Just a line to let you know how we spent Christmas. At midnight on Christmas Eve, ALL THE FIRING STOPPED. On Christmas morning we were walking on the top of our trenches.

The Germans started to walk up to our trenches, so we met them halfway. We gave them cigarettes & they gave us some cigars. Our papers say they are not getting enough food. From what I saw of them I do not think they are starved".

He concludes saying how hard it is being in the trenches for 21 days, & could they send him his watch, as the only one they had in the trench got broken the other day.

By a strange irony of fate the following week (January 14th), the Mail reported

Rifleman Goodey of 9 Balliol Road, Reading Street was being relieved after four weeks in the trenches, where he escaped unhurt. Making his way to the village for a well earned rest, a sniper hit him, wounding him so seriously he speedily expired.

Rifleman Goodey was a promising lad of nineteen & had given proof on two occasions of his bravery & fearlessness in the presence of danger.

Back in Broadstairs, volunteers for the services were still being asked for. Those that were at this stage unable or unwilling were asked to join the Broadstairs Volunteer Training Corps, which was an early form of the Home Guard. All of the local groups were affiliated to the Central Association of Volunteers & came under the War Office. Essentially it was made up of businessmen, the medically unfit, & the over & under age for the services. As part of signing on everyman had to declare that he would do his duty, which made the Volunteer units a hunting ground for raw recruits into the Army. The cut off age was 38, & under that age you could posted anywhere thought necessary. Many of the Broadstairs volunteers ended up patrolling the docks at Chatham, or on the banks of the Thames doing guard duty.

The Broadstairs Unit met once a week at the Grand Pavilion in Westcliff Road, where they were schooled in drill & rifle maintenance. Other duties were to assist the special constables which were up to 30 in number by this time.

A frequently asked question was finally answered by the council of the 9th January.

IF BOMBARDED
Instructions as to what the population of Broadstairs is to do in case of bombardment, or an attempt to land a hostile force. It has been thought that the inhabitants would be glad to know that the military preparations have already been made in the event of any contingency occurring.

1 IN CASE OF BOMBARDMENT the civil population is advised to keep indoors & take shelter in the cellars or the lowest rooms in the house.

2 IN CASE OF INVASION should news reach the inhabitants that a landing is to be attempted or has been effected, they are enjoined to remain quietly in their home.

No movement will take place without authority. If it should be thought advisable by the Military Authorities that the district should be immediately vacated, instructions will be immediately communicated to the inhabitants through the Police or Special Constabulary. Such instructions will inform the people where they should go, & by what road.

Frank Brightman
Chairman Broadstairs & St Peters Urban District Council
9th January 1915.

Wanted!

400 People to Subscribe £1 each to equip the BROADSTAIRS AND ST. PETER'S VOLUNTEERS, and prepare them for the task of defending our British Homes.

January 27th
RIFLES FOR RAILWAYMEN

Through the generosity of Colonel Colin Campbell of "Port Regis", who is serving at the Front, he has sent Mr Rigden, the Broadstairs Stationmaster at Broadstairs a gift of three Morris tube miniature rifles of the latest type complete with magazines, orthoptics, & 1,000 rounds of ammunition. These rifles the Colonel has intended to be given to the members of the staff for practice. On hearing of the news the Rev F G Ridgeway has given a donation to help defray the expenses. Mr Rigden, who will supervise his staff, is a member of the Training Volunteer Corps, & is a crack shot.

Messrs H Cooper & Co, the Council contractors for supplying granite & macadam wrote to the Council stating they were unable to get a barge to transport granite chippings for the roads, owing to the military & naval situation.

February 3rd   THE YOUNG DEFENDERS- AN APPEAL

Broadstairs Scouts work since the start of the war
It will undoubtedly prove interesting to the townspeople to know what the local Scouts have been doing since war broke out.
Since last August about twenty of them have been doing night duty at the Gasworks & Water undertaking, & other important places in the town. They have now surrendered these duties to the recently appointed special constables. The Scouts have been meeting once a week at the Grand Pavilion, but have

relinquished their meetings to the local Volunteer Training Corps since they have been set up. They have been meeting recently at Pierremont Hall.

During the last three months the Troop have gained forty proficiency badges, & could have gained more if they had a suitable headquarters. They have now accepted an empty house in St Peters, which they hope to convert, & for which they have appealed for funds.

The Scouts are an old organisation in the town, & hope, amongst the many new organisations, that they won't be forgotten.

On February 3rd the first six monthly report of the Councils Emergency Committee was issued.

The Committee has been actively involved with all the problems associated with the war relief on the home front. When recruits are called up, if they are married or have dependants, adequate financial provision has been made whilst the breadwinner was away on active service. The Soldiers & Sailors Association has been looking after the administration side of the business.

The Separation Allowance is 12/6d per week for a wife For a wife & child 15/-, Wife & two children 17/6d, & 2/- for every additional child over four years of age.

Since August Broadstairs & St Peters has donated £303 to the Prince of Wales Fund £103 alone being collected by the town's churches & chapels. £150 has been distributed as relief to around 100 families, the Red Cross V A D has received £92.17s, The Belgian Fund £53.16s the Queens Work for Women £33.3s, to name a few organisation that have benefited. The Ladies Working Party Committee have spent £47.8.11d on purchasing materials for making mittens, comforters, balaclavas, socks etc. Clothing for the Belgian wounded has also been supplied mainly for Fairfield & Roseneath. Their actions have been highly praised by the Belgian recipients. The work is ongoing & materials, funds, & volunteers are always needed.

Enterprising boys have been collecting walking sticks for the wounded, one lad having collected fifty six so far.

The patrolling of the local volunteers & soldiers did not always go according to plan.

February 3rd   MYSTERIOUS AFFAIR AT KINGSGATE
A night search
A strange tale of an attack by three men on a soldier near the "Captain Digby".

The victim of the affair was Lance Corporal Richardson of "A" Company Kent Cyclists Brigade stationed at the "Digby". At about 10.20 last Monday night, he was on duty when he was attacked by three men, & was knocked down & repeatedly kicked. In spite of the odds, he managed to regain his feet, & the assailants bolted, but not before Richardson had received a wound in the left knee from the upward thrust of a knife.

Richardson then raised the alarm & eleven of his colleagues with the Coastguards & the Police set out in search of the perpetrators, & after a considerable time scouring the district, ultimately ceased their errand.

The Police have been unable to solve the mystery, & are baffled by the extraordinary circumstances of the attack.

The stories of spies abound in the town.

Another incident occurred on February 24th

SENTRIES MIRACULOUS ESCAPE

A remarkable accident occurred at Dumpton Gap in the small hours of Saturday morning, when Private William Searson & Private Arthur Clark, both of the 8th Battalion Kings Own Liverpool Regiment narrowly escaped injury when about 40 tons of cliff fell where they were doing guard duty. Private Clark escaped injury, but Searson was buried under the falling chalk. Although entombed for over two hours he was found suffering from nothing more than shock & bruising.

Clark who managed to see what was coming, darted out of the way, but Searson was less fortunate & was completely buried until he was dug out two & a half hours later. Clark called for assistance & with the help of a coastguard & several other soldiers managed to dig him out. After he was extracted he was taken to the Whittuck Home where he is billeted. Dr F Brightman was called & declared Searson fit after some rest. The Gap is now partially blocked & a large number of visitors have viewed the scene. The Council Surveyor has now had the debris removed.

On February 10th, the question of preparing a Roll of Honour was suggested by Councillor Brightman. This was to commemorate all those who had responded to the Countries call. He thought the town should have a suitable list of all those who had given their services, & with the co-operation of the Council & the townspeople, they could get all the names together, & have them displayed in a public position in the town. The suggestion met with the full support of the Council.

Another suggestion came from Mr W N Ross, Company Commandant of the Broadstairs & St Peters Training Corps.

TRENCHES ON THE FORESHORE

Commander Ross has asked the Council if it would give permission for the Corps to practice trench digging on the main sands at Broadstairs, & lend them the necessary implements to carry out the work. Any damage done would be made good by the corps. They also requested a proper rifle range to be built either in the newly acquired Pierremont Park or at the football ground at Dumpton Park.

The Council have turned the idea of the rifle range down as both sites are in too public a place.

The Councillors thought that digging up the foreshore to be a reasonable suggestion & were generally agreeable, until Councillor Moodey suggested that perhaps they had lost sight of the possibility that the London papers might say about trenches being dug on Broadstairs sands & thought they ought to think about it a bit more.

They did, & Commandant Ross was turned down on both suggestions.

One week later the Mail came up with the suggestion of using the Broadstairs & St Peters Training Corps to dig up the lower High Street.

One suggestion that did get carried out was put foreword by Councillor Pemble.

WHITEWASHING THE KERBS

Councillor Pemble suggested that as the town was now in virtual darkness in the evenings, whether they should consider whitewashing the kerbs to eliminate the possibility of accidents. A number of people had already fallen down as there was nothing to indicate where the kerbs were when it was dark. *"Good idea"*, said a voice, *"that will help the drunks find their way home"*.

The surveyor was instructed to experiment with spent lime from Rumfields, (brickworks), & Portland cement grout, making a start on the street corners first.

After painting the kerbs, it rained solidly for a week, & most of the "paint" became a *"gluttonous mess"*, which had to be done again, *"use paint this time"*, said one Councillor.

On February the 24th the Councillors met Military representatives in the town. This was as a result of the petition sent to the Military Authorities at the end of last year. The meeting was to investigate how many soldiers could be billeted in the town if necessary. Although nothing definite has been arranged, the Chairman thought the ratepayers should know what progress had been made.

An amusing incident took place on the 10th of April, which could have had a disastrous result.
RESCUE OF TERRITORIAL OFF NORTH FORELAND.
On Thursday morning, at about 11 o'clock, the exciting rescue of one of the Kent Cyclists, stationed at the Captain Digby was effected off the North Foreland. The boat in which the soldier had gone out in, was about two miles off shore & was spotted through field glasses by the guard of the Kings Own Liverpool Regiment, stationed at the North Foreland. The occupant was seen to be in difficulties, & a boat was put off from Joss Bay containing Sergeant Dickenson, Corporal White. & Privates Banks & Austen. A crowd quickly appeared on the beach which included the Coastguards & members of the Cyclists Battalion, who arrived on bicycles.

After a hard pull out to the unfortunate Territorial, he was reached & transferred to the rescuers boat, apparently none the worse for his adventurous trip. It appears that the boat he had gone off in was no more than a canoe, propelled by nothing other than a spade.

The Liverpools are to be congratulated on their stirling rescue.

Broadstairs & St Peters Echo

After much debate, the Council decided to go ahead with the summer entertainments, "*If we leave the decision any later, then we might as well all go to the Front*", was one retort. All the usual concessions were put out to tender, & everything would carry on as near to normal as possible. Civilian bands were organised to play at the bandstand, & a license was applied for to play in the Pierremont Gardens. "Uncle Mack" had been organised to play at his pitch on the beach & the pier in the evenings, Oliver Marsh had replaced three of his forty bathing machines, & all the concessions for newspapers, fruit selling, & photography had been snapped up. The subject was again raised about taking photographs of people in bathing costumes, & touting for business on the promenade came up, both were banned as they were last year. Professor Spencer even got permission to conduct swimming lessons from the sands; the Council had turned him down before.

The pier head, clock shelter & bandstand were all to be repainted, as soon as weather & tenders allowed.

THE LIGHT THAT WAS TOO BRIGHT

Fanny Collinson of the Albion Hotel was summoned at the Cinque Ports Court on Monday for not obscuring the lights at the hotel.

Special Constable Rudland said he saw two bright lights on the second floor; one was quite visible from the sea. This was in no way obscured & the blind was not drawn. The other one was a strong light behind a red curtain. The defendant expressed her regret.

The Bench considered the case, & reminded her that she was open to a fine of £100 or 6 months imprisonment. They dealt with her leniently & fined her £5.

Two weeks later

At the Cinque Ports Petty Sessions Neville William Ross of Pierremont Hall was summoned for an offence under the lighting order.

Police Sergeant Hadaway said he was on duty on the 14th, & at 9pm he saw bright lights on at the Hall. He informed the defendant he would be reported. Mr Ross replied he had 75 windows & 6 maids at the house & they must have neglected to obscure the lights. He was fined £5.

Mr Ross is Commandant of the Broadstairs Volunteer Training Corps.

On the subject of lighting, Mr J H Summerson, "Uncle Mack", wrote from London & drew the Councils attention to the fact that objections would be raised if the pier was to be lighted during his evening's performances during the summer season. Could they possible find him another venue for the evening performance? The council thought it would be OK till August & they'd see what happened after that.

On 28th April, additions were added to the Aliens Restriction Act of 1914, & came into force immediately.

It is the duty of every keeper or manager of a lodging or boarding house, hotel, inn or apartment, to keep a register of all aliens over the age of 14 years staying in the house. Every person staying in the house should also have a signed statement showing their nationality. The penalty for failure to do so is £100 or six months imprisonment.

Also in April, the Government was in touch with all of the councils, requesting them to release all available manual workers for war duty. After calling a meeting with the few remaining workers it still had, the Council left it to the men to decide.

NAVY LETTER TO THE COUNCIL

Lieutenant Commander Dewer, has enclosed a copy of his authority to Mr Ross, the Company Commandant of the Broadstairs Volunteer Training Corps, requesting him to set up a watch on Broadstairs Harbour from 9pm till 6am each night. On behalf of the Senior Naval Authority, Mr Ross requested the Council to grant permission for the Training Corps to use the Droit Office as a base. (Mr Ross had been in trouble with Council before after damage was done to the fireplace in the Droit Office after he last used it. This time he had to use superior authority to get his way). *The Council stipulated that they would provide coal, gas, chairs & cleaning utensils at a cost of 10/- per week & the Naval Authorities to make good any damage.*

Mr Ross insisted on a meeting with a Council representative to survey & complete an inventory of the Droit Office before he used it.

The Corps by now numbered over 100, & the Council asked, what would be the position of the men in the Corps if there was a serious attempt to land? They have no uniforms, & in the eyes of the enemy they would probably be taken for spies. Should we not have an all out effort & attempt to purchase the equipment these men should have? An incident followed a few nights later when two patrolling Specials, were held up on the approach to the pier, by two men in civvies with a revolver. It turned out that they were over enthusiastic members of the Training Corps, & the only distinguishing features was an arm band on the Specials, & a small badge on the Training Corps, neither being able to be seen in the dark.

By May 19th all the Volunteers were in uniform.

GERMAN AIRSHIP DROP BOMBS ON TOWN May 19th

The Mail covered in great detail the first zeppelin raid that took place on Ramsgate at 1.48am on the Monday morning of May 17th, when about 25 incendiary devices were dropped on the town.

A Special Constable, who was on duty in Victoria Gardens in Broadstairs said, about 1.30am he observed a dark object in the sky coming from the Margate direction. It was not travelling very fast, but made a loud noise. It passed over the middle of the town going towards Ramsgate. He watched it, & saw flashes of light being thrown onto the dark object, changing it into a silver colour.

Mr Whitehead, an engine driver at Rumfields Pumping Station, told of the peculiar movements of the machine before making for Ramsgate.

"About 1.45, I saw the zeppelin coming over from Margate. West of the pumping station the engine of the zeppelin stopped, restarting several minutes later when the pilot appeared to alter course to the south east. When first seen it was travelling very slowly, but after altering course the speed greatly increased."

At St Peters & Reading Street the noise made by the zeppelin was heard, & many residents gathered in the street to watch the airship go over.

After the raid the zeppelin was chased by machines, (aircraft), from Westgate & Eastchurch as far as the West Hinder Lightship. When off Nieuport she was attacked by eight naval machines from Dunkirk, who attacked her at close range. Four bombs were dropped from 200 feet above the airship by Flight Commander Bigsworth & a large column of smoke was seen to come from her compartment. The zeppelin then rose to a great height of 11,000 feet, with her tail down, badly damaged. All eight of our aircraft came under heavy fire.

It would appear the Broadstairs & Margate had a lucky escape.

The following week the local tradesmen started to change their newspaper adverts. It was now possible to buy KYL FYRE Extinguishers, (Prepare for Zeppelins), at Harringtons in York Street

---

H. E. HARRINGTON,
(Successor to F. K. DODD)
General & Furnishing Ironmonger.

Prepare for Zeppelins!
KYL-FYRE EXTINGUISHERS
5/6 cash.

1, York Street, Broadstairs.
TELEPHONE 91.

& D T Evans were ready with their special respirators on sale in the High Street.

> June 19, 1915.
>
> ✕
>
> **SPECIAL**
>
> # RESPIRATORS
>
> (As approved by the War Office) for Protection against
>
> # POISONOUS
> # GERMAN GASES
>
> are obtainable at
>
> # D. T. EVANS,
>
> Dispensing Chemist,
>
> 5, HIGH STREET, BROADSTAIRS.
>
> Also at
> Margate, Ramsgate, Westgate and Birchington.
>
> *Special Solution for use with Home-made Respirators in 1/- Bottles.*
>
> ✕

WOUNDED AT BROADSTAIRS

Every praise is due in the manner in which the Red Cross workers handled the wounded men who were brought into Ramsgate last weekend. There is not the slightest hitch in the arrangements at the station, & in a very short space of time; the men are tucked up in bed in various hospitals.

Seventy men were detrained at Ramsgate, sixty of them being brought to the Yarrow Home & Fairfield House. During the time they have been there the skilful nursing has already made itself felt, & comforts have been lavished on them every day by the hospital staff & visitors who call to see them.

Some of the men could, with difficulty, speak of their many adventures. Sergeant Gower of the 1st Batt Royal Irish Fusiliers, is suffering from frostbite & bronchitis, & told our reporter, "I have been out there since August & thought it wouldn't last much longer. The Germans are getting fed up with it".

Gower had met with the Kaisers much vaunted Bavarian troops near Messines. He was convinced they would give up if they knew they would be looked after by the British. They had been told by their officers that they would be shot by the British if they were captured. They are running out of supplies & have not fired a shot since Christmas. We sometimes get out of the trenches when it's dark & run around to keep warm. The cold & damp were the only things we were suffering from.

"It was an awful shame to see some of the beautiful houses all totally wrecked, magnificent places some of them. Some of the locals are still working in the fields & are expert in telling the difference in the shells, whether their German, French or the allies, as they whistle overhead."

On the food front, he said some of the men soaked their biscuits in water & then fried them in bacon fat, "& very nice they are to". The most extraordinary use for biscuits he said was as fuel for fires in the trenches. Sergeant Gower explained "they burnt with a clear hot flame rather like charcoal giving out a great deal of heat".

Keeping the troops amused was some thing the people of Broadstairs were good at

CONCERT AT THE YARROW HOME.

On Sunday a concert was organised by Mr Swiney for the British invalids at the Yarrow Home. Items were rendered by the following artistes Miss E Harding, Miss B Ryder, Miss D Webb, & Mr James Avon. They were accompanied on the piano. The troops harmoniously joined in with some glee singing. After a short interval during which cigarettes were distributed amongst the soldiers, the following pictures were shown.

"The Fatal Taxi Cab", the amusing Keystone Comics, whose antics caused much merriment & a travel film "On the River Marne" was followed by "Castle", an Edison drama which came in two parts. At the conclusion Mmlle Denise sang "La Marseillaise" in French, with limelight effects. This was followed by a rousing performance of the National Anthem.

Broadstairs had been a largely alien free town since early on in the war; those that did stay were well registered & documented under the Aliens Act. Virtually all of the Belgian refugees that had arrived were moved further inland away from the coast. Any business in the town with the remotest of foreign sounding name was quickly targeted, which brought about the following advert in the Echo.

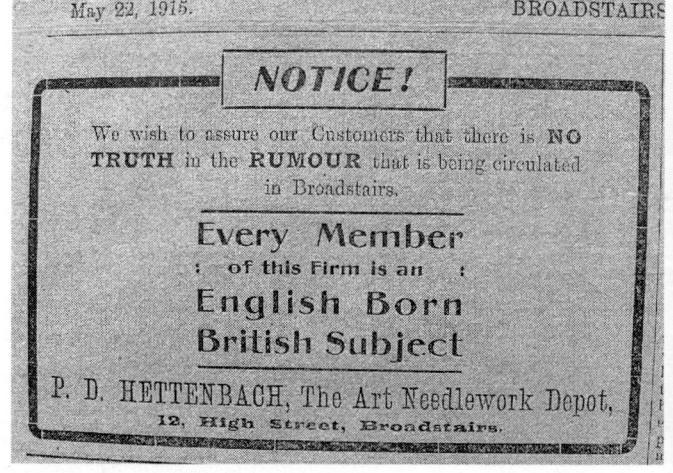

WOMENS PLACE IN THE WAR

There is an advertisement in this paper for women clerks in an office, where there is a shortage of staff owing to the war. The war has brought about the introduction of women in the workplace which has traditionally been an all male preserve. Women have always taken a prominent role in certain branches of business life notably schools, hospitals & boarding houses. The woman clerk is a familiar figure in large commercial premises, but not so far seen in Thanet. Women have so far not taken to driving motors for hire, or deliveries, though the number of women drivers is becoming more noticeable. There are women now in shops which was once the sole domain of men before the war, & other suggestions have been carriage cleaners on the railway, ticket collectors, luggage porters, & tram conductors, & lots of other similar positions that would release more men into the armed services.

Up to the present the work behind the counter & of the distribution of groceries & provisions has been confined to men, but employees now have to experiment with engaging lady assistants, which on the whole has been a successful one. The Broadstairs manager of one branch of a multiple firm now has a few lady assistants, "They all have to be trained or course" he said, "& were naturally very slow at first. It took three of them to do the work of one man, & it was badly done at that", explained the manager, "Still they are willing, clean, & neat, & after a short time will make ideal assistants". He had been instructed by head office not to employ any men of military age. This is visible proof that the women of Great Britain realise to the full their responsibilities.

Broadstairs & St Peters Mail 2nd June 1915

Two weeks later

A BROADSTAIRS FIRST

Broadstairs Station has the novel distinction of having the first lady ticket collector in Thanet. Miss Mullinger has commenced her duties this week. The appearance of a member of the fairer sex in uniform on the railway platform has arrested much attention. Through her appointment she has allowed another railwayman to be released for military service. In the goods department, Miss Stevens has been appointed the first lady railway clerk.

Dressed in blue serge, Miss Mullinger has made an exceptionally smart appearance. The coat & skirt are made in the Norfolk style with military cut pockets & gold buttons. The S E C R badge in gold braid is attached to each coat collar. A peaked cap is worn with an oak leaf band.

Miss Mullinger has received several weeks training at Ashford.

The Mail commented, "We anticipate with great excitement the first train driven by a lady train driver."

(Eight weeks later, on the 1st September, Miss Mullinger transferred to Margate & was succeeded at Broadstairs by Miss Alice Elgar.)

The Council had warning sirens fitted to the water tower at Rumfields, the tram depot in Northdown Road, & on the fire station at the Broadway. These were to be sounded in case of an air raid, but very few instructions appear to have been issued as to what to do if they sounded.

After one practice sounding, the letters of complaint started to roll in

> Sir
>
> After last nights practice it is hoped that the Authorities at Broadstairs are satisfied with the scaring effect of the new syren fitted at Rumfields. Is it really necessary for the noise to be continued for the same length of time whenever a reputed hostile aircraft is reported within 20 miles of us? Surely it would be equally effective & far less alarming if some well known tune as "Rule Britannia" could be played.

The local newspapers published the weekly schedules for the Local Volunteer Force. In May of 1915 the Broadstairs & St Peters Company was kept busy.

> Monday 8 till 9 Inspection by Capt P Dampier at the Banks
> Monday 6.30 till 9 Section 1 Range construction. Platoon Sergeant Gatland in charge
> Range Tues., Wed, Thurs, Sat 7 till 7 Ladies, 9.30 members drill
> Tuesday 8 till 9 Platoon 2, 3, Section 2, Range Construction Platoon Sergeant Brett in charge
> Wednesday 8 till 9 Signalling Class, 6.30 till 9 Sections 3,4,5,6, Range Construction Platoon Sergeant Hooker in charge.
> Thursday 7.15 Platoon 1 The Banks, (Bairds Hill), 8.30 till 9 Range Construction
> Reminder Sunday May 23rd General Muster, Parade, & route march

The Sergeant in Charge of Construction of the Range MUST see that he signs the book provided by the Council, for the receipt of the tools kindly lent by the Council, & see that the caretaker signs for the *return of the same. Planks, Barrows may be borrowed from the builders on the ground, but they must be returned when done with. In no circumstances may planks be taken from the scaffolding of the buildings.*

Neville Ross Company Commander

By the 6th of June the new rifle range behind Crampton Tower was completed. The first shot was fired by Mrs Ross, wife of the Volunteers Force Commander. *The range is in the open air, & the Corps are indebted to the council for the loan of the ground.* A mound of earth was raise 36 feet long, 20 feet wide & 13 feet 6 inches high to accept the target area. Shooting was only to be allowed in the evenings, after the new Council School, (St Mildreds), opened on June 23rd.

New lighting regulations were brought in on the 14th July. No street lights of any form were allowed to be shown in any coastal town. There was to be no lights shown externally from any buildings. All internal lights had to be obscured from the outside.

This caused the traders to shut their shops at 7pm each evening, rather that the 8.30 or 9pm when they had been shutting under normal circumstances. By the winter of 1915, the shops were shutting at 5 pm but the Council allowed them to stay open throughout the lunch period.

SHOP EARLY.
Customers are requested to shop before dark in order that we may comply with the Lighting Regulations.

Phone 6x **H. G. WATSON,** Phone 6x
GENERAL & FURNISHING IRONMONGER,
CHINA & GLASS WAREHOUSE,

Thanet Useful Stores,
ST. PETER'S ROAD & SOWELL STREET,

General Household Repairs.

The Mail was often printing locals' poetry, a favourite occupation in the evenings, often commenting on the events of the day.

PUT THAT LIGHT OUT

When the dusk is softly falling
& the darkness wraps in doubt,
Busy street & obscure alley
& you don't know who's about
Then the pop'lar phrase is rampant
Heard in whisper then a shout
Where' ere you go it seems to follow
    "Put that light out".

Maybe you've just succeeded
After a long & weary roam
In the pitchy, inky darkness,
To arrive safely in your home
By the aid of a ½d rushlight
Try to read what K's about,
Then comes the raucous order
    "Put that light out".

Since you had a motorbike,
Some fines you had to pay,
For riding it without lights
Upon the Kings Highway,
So you fixed it with a beacon
That shone for miles around
Now you're fined because you didn't
    "Put that light out".

Oh for houses without windows
In these days of the Huns,
Without doors & without keyholes
To attract their little bombs,
You must dwell in such a dwelling
Even out at Lydden's Spout
If you could only escape the watchword
    "Put that light out"

On June 23rd, under the Chairman of the Council, the Assembly Rooms, (Charles Dickens P H), at Nuckells Place, were converted into a recreation & reading room for convalescing servicemen. *There is an appeal out in the town for newspapers, periodicals, magazines, books, draughts, dominoes & cards. Mr Blackburn has donated furniture, Mr Hempstead crockery, Mr H Strevens, books, & Mr J T May a sink for the canteen.*

Sand Bags !
Sand Bags !!
Sand Bags !!!

White Rose League

United Women's Patriotic White Rose Clubs.

Walls of Sand Bags are Needed !

Sand Bags are as much needed as Munitions.

It takes 100,000 Sandbags for a 1 mile Trench, although the War Office send one million a month, millions more are required. The White Rose League send these bags passed by the ordnance **Direct to the Front.** Carriage paid by Authorites. The Work is all **Voluntary.** Soldiers and Sailors wives at the 6 White Rose Centres in Manchester and London give their work FREE. There are 600 helpers.

On Sand Bag Procession Day an officer threw in £1 saying " A Thank Offering," Sand Bags saved his life.

Letters of appeal are received DAILY by the White Rose League from the Front.

"Send us Sand Bags" £1 makes 64 complete.

Large Airy Work Rooms at White Rose Club, 199, High Street, Notting Hill Gate, London. The first White Rose Club was opened by **Lord Kitchener's Sister, Mrs. Parker.**

SANDBAGS

The Vicar of St Peters Church, observes, "There is a great need, almost an unlimited demand, for sandbags for the soldiers at the Front. Working parties are held at the Vicarage, & elsewhere in the town. Miss Nicholls is working very enthusiastically on this cause & donations to purchase materials are urgently called for. Every sandbag may be the means of saving life of our boys at the Front,

Money should be sent to Miss Nicholls, Kingsdown Farm at Bromstone, or to Miss Mathews at the Vicarage. To date (August), 2119 sandbags have been made at a cost of £9.15s.

This brought a query as to how can anyone make 2,119 sandbags for £9.15s. It was explained that the material bought cost £5 for 500 feet as surplus material, & the rest was donated.

Mrs Cooper of Reading Street was also active on the sandbag making front, & received a letter thanking her & her band of workers for their help, "*Ask the people to put a prayer in the bags for the men who are risking their lives*". Over 1,100 had been sent from the workers at St Andrews in Reading Street.

ROYAL MARINES CONCERT
July 7th

The band of the Royal Marines played at the newly laid out Pierremont Gardens. The audience was made up of a mixture of wounded servicemen & visitors. Over 700 patrons listened to the band performing at the temporary bandstand erected for the event.

On the first anniversary of the start of the war, (on 4th August 1915), it was announced that Broadstairs & St Peters, including Reading Street, had sent a total of 460 men into the Army & associated services & 100 more had gone into the Navy. There were 130 Special Constables recruited in Broadstairs, & 610 men had enrolled in the Volunteer Training Reserve.

On August the 4th, new motor vehicle lighting regulations were introduced. These orders were for all vehicles, buses, cars & motorcycles,
- A) Motor vehicles using oil lamps or candles, no change.
- B) Motorcycles burning electric head lights not to exceed 25 candle power. Side & rear lights not to exceed 8 candle power.
- C) Motor vehicles using acetylene lighting, as above in B
- D) All reflectors to be dull-blackened
- E) Upper portion of all glasses to ½" below halfway, to be dull-blackened.

The Specials had a field day with the lighting regulations, particularly with anyone in authority. On average there were ten prosecutions a week for lighting offences in Broadstairs. Most got away with a £1 fine & costs, a few were made an example of & were fined £5.

In August the Government implemented the National Registration Act, where everyone would be documented as in a census, (the last one was in 1911). Apart from the usual name, age, & address, a lot of emphasis was put on occupation & medical condition. Many saw this as a precursor to conscription, & ordinance manufacture. The *Broadstairs & St Peters Echo* commented, "*The National Register, which has for so long been in every ones mind, has come at last. By this time every house in the district has received a visit from an enumerator, who must be a very long suffering person.* (There was more than one). *In the daily newspapers instructions have been given upon filling up the forms, & the whole gigantic task will probably be accomplished smoothly & accurately. There still remains one question, the chief one of all, which is still in doubt. There are many theories as to what the information secured will be put. Many believe that it is merely the forerunner of compulsory service. This is as it may be, but it would be a very wise man, or a very foolish one, to express a definite opinion either for or against this view. But to provide against all contingencies, I would advise all young men, who have no ties, to join the colours now. If, as a result of the register or any other measure, compulsory service is adopted, they will most probably find the rate of pay very different to what it is now under the voluntary system*".

Up till July 10th, 465 men from Broadstairs, St Peters & environs, were serving in the forces. By December 1915, this had grown to 582.

The *Echo* also reported in August, that the "White Feather Brigade" had descended on Broadstairs. Individual, or usually groups of ladies, would accost a young man in the street if he was not wearing a service armlet, & present him with a white feather. This was usually done in the most public place possible, & was an attempt to shame the young man into enlisting.

A Bradstonian, who had fought at Mons, & was invalided out of the service, had a white feather stuck in his buttonhole the other day whilst in the High Street. The lady refused to accept any of his explanations, so he said he'd keep the feather as a souvenir anyway. The Echo reported, "*& we endorse all his remarks said about the "White Feather Brigade". For young men to be walking down the street & have a white feather thrust into their faces, by young ladies who knows absolutely nothing about them, is both obnoxious & objectionable in the extreme. Women are doing excellent service for this country at this time of war, & I am sure their energies can be better spent than blackguarding young fellows into enlistment. Let us try gentle persuasion & appeal to a young man's honour, not insult him*".

Many tactics were used to persuade men to enlist. At one recruiting rally in Broadstairs, the speaker turned the tables & spoke to the young women in the audience. "*Think about it young ladies, is that man by you side really worth it. He's still here, not doing his duty for either King or Country. Will he do his duty by you, will you let him go? Make a man of him, & persuade him to volunteer, he'll be the better for it, & so will you*".

The usual rounds of harvest festivals took place at the end of September. The Rev C Cowland Cooper of St Andrews in Reading Street, decided that instead of having the usual display of vegetable &

flowers, (which would be welcome anyway), that this year they would display & then give socks, mufflers, cigarettes & sweets to the soldiers at the Front.

A SOLDIER AT 14

Drummer E Jarman of the 2nd Battalion of the Buffs, although not 15 years old, has been at the Front since June. He enlisted at Ramsgate in February, stating that his age was 18. When his proper age was discovered, he was discharged, & arrived home at 14 Upton Road last Friday, (15th September). Though he had spent most of his time in the trenches, he had never been under any attack. Asked whether he was nervous when he went first into the firing line, he said" Yes at first, but after a time took no notice of it". Though he had seen many men killed, he was sorry to leave the Army as he liked the life.

A RUSSIAN DECORATION FOR A BROADSTAIRS SOLDIER   22nd September

A further honour has been conferred on Corporal H W Hill, 1st Battalion of the Buffs, who has already been mentioned in Sir John French's despatches, for which he has received the D C M. It is announced that the Czar of Russia has granted him a 2nd Class St George medal, which is a rare distinction. No definite details have been announced as yet, but it is thought that Corporal Hill went out, at considerable personal risk, & cut the German's communication wires. He returned to the Front in July after an attack of enteric fever. Corporal Hills is 22 years old.

On 22nd September Neville Ross the Commander of the Broadstairs Volunteer Reserve Force, & headmaster of Pierremont College, offered his services to the War Office, & was made a 2nd Lieutenant of no particular regiment. Because of his fluency in German, he was made an interpreter, based at Stopps Castle in Scotland, interviewing German Prisoners of War. The new Commander of the V R F at Broadstairs was Mr H T Gullick of "The Banks" Bairds Hill, the Platoon Commander was to be Mr C S Reed.

A petition was sent to the Council by the tradesmen of the town about a query relating to compensation over any airborne damage that might occur in the town. the advice they had been given, after the Ramsgate bombing, was that there would not be any government compensation, & therefore the only way to rebuild their damaged properties would be to take out expensive insurance to cover the event. They thought this was wrong, as it was a National problem & not one restricted to the east coast towns.

The Council was sympathetic, & joined other towns in lobbying Parliament.

As the autumn nights turned into winter, the Council started painting white bands around pillar boxes, & trees. There had been many accidents to pedestrians colliding with street furniture in the dark. A request also went out to the Gas Company to do the same for the street lights, & the Electric Light & Tram Company to paint white bands round the tram standards & the electric light posts.

Another idea that quickly spread throughout Thanet was the War Discs.

13th Oct   *WAR DISCS FOR PATRIOTIC HOUSEHOLDERS*

Every street in Broadstairs is displaying a new war disc, "Not At Home". This has spread throughout Thanet, & signifies that from the house, in which it is displayed, a man has gone into the services.

In Ramsgate many houses are showing a remarkable display, showing three or four discs, an eloquent testimony of the response that, that town has made to the patriotic call.

The discs are being distributed by the Soldiers, & Sailors Families Association, & we are told that the record locally is one house in Cliffsend showing seven discs.

SACRIFICIAL FIRES

Commencing from Monday next, a new order of things will begin in Broadstairs. The Council has intimated by hand bills distributed in the town, that the collection of private house refuse will only be made on Monday, Wednesday, Friday & Saturday of each week. Householders are requested to burn all paper, cardboard, & straw. This is best done on a bonfire in the backyard, a method that will no doubt be adopted in most instances. With regard to trade waste the Council will NOT collect straw, paper, cardboard, shavings & any bulky items, & tradesmen must find some other method of removing the rubbish themselves.

Broadstairs & St Peters Echo 16th Oct 1915

KENT MEN IN GERMANY October 27th

There was a report issued by Mr Spoor (of the Red Cross), on the plight of the men imprisoned in German prison camps. These men were broken down & scarcely a week went by without a report that another of their Kentish men was dead & buried. As they come home, all the prisoners said the food sent out to them was all that kept them alive. The difficulty was in keeping in touch with the men as they were continually being shuffled around Germany. He could ensure everybody, who sent out parcels the men, received everything that was sent out.

Mr Spoor pointed out that the men were only allowed to send one postcard home a week. When it was written, it was held up for scrutiny for ten days by the German authorities before being forwarded. The Germans were very suspicious of certain symbols such as X, which they thought of as some form of secret code.

Mr Spoor submitted a list of suitable stuffs for sending which includes jam, margarine, dripping, marmalade, syrup, cocoa powder, tea, coffee, corned beef, oxo cubes, salt, pepper, biscuits, Sunlight soap, Quaker oats, condensed milk, & vegetables in tins. He reiterated the fact that the Germans were now willing to accept food in tins.

He said that some of the men were fed with red herrings, which they couldn't get on with, & after they had played cricket or football with them, they were handed over to the Russian P O W's, who considered them to be a tasty relish.

Mr Spoor said he was able to get cigarettes & tobacco at bond prices, tobacco being 1s 6d a pound. Matches were only to be sent in hermetically sealed tins. About 80% of the bread sent out was either stale or mouldy when it arrived. A special box, to take two 2lb loaves was now available from a firm in Chatham, & the post was only 9d.

He went on to thank all those who had contributed in all their various ways, of doing their bit for the unfortunate men who are overseas.

The good ladies of Broadstairs & St Peters were well aware of the good work they were doing. Ably assisted by the girls of the various schools in the town, the food parcels & knitting circles were always kept busy. Not only were they looking after their own men who were away, they also adopted servicemen who had been billeted in the town, & the wounded on their return to the Yarrow Home, Fairfield or Roseneath hospitals. Those who couldn't make or cook were put to use organising concert parties for either the invalid servicemen or raising money for the materials funds.

The ladies were always thinking ahead, & the Mail in October carried the headline

CHRISTMAS PUDDINGS FOR EVERY BROADSTAIRS P O W

Several kind offers of Christmas puddings for inclusion into parcels will now be packed on November 1st. It now appears that they will not arrive in good condition unless packed in hermetically sealed tins. Puddings specially prepared, can be obtained from big stores, Vyes, & the International Tea Stores. Mrs Hugh Raven will be glad to receive any offers.

Odd items were requested at times from the men. One group of Buffs requested a football to relieve the boredom. Harmonicas were also another frequently requested item. Some troops aimed high, another group requested a gramophone, *"We have some old records in a house to play on it"*. Arthur Lurock of the 1st/2nd Field Ambulance wrote to the Mail, *"Can any reader oblige by sending an old accordion or concertina to pass our dreary evenings away. Perhaps it will drown out the incessant sound of the heavy artillery".*

XMAS PRESENTS FOR BROADSTAIRS P O W

The parcels were packed by the committee at Mr Fosters in Sowell Street. They consisted of one pot of jam, one marmalade, one tin of coffee, one of sardines, one of cocoa, one of milk, one of chocolate, one ginger, one Oxo, two soup tablets, one xmas pudding, one tin of meat, ½ lb of tea, two potted meats, 1 lb biscuits, 1 lb margarine, pepper, salt, mustard, one packet of tobacco, one cardigan, one bodybelt, one pair of mittens, & one new shirt.

Wanted! MEN for the MECHANICAL TRANSPORT of the Army Service Corps.

A MECHANICAL TRANSPORT OFFICER will attend at the Recruiting Office, Depot—The Buffs, CANTERBURY, on THURSDAY, OCT. 28th, for the purpose of accepting suitable men for Service in the above Corps.

Candidates should have at least one year's driving experience, and should be used to driving Cars or Lorries with gate change.

Men desirous of joining the above Corps should present themselves between the hours of 12 and 5 o'clock, and bring with them testimonials and references.

Candidates should apply to the nearest Recruiting Office for a Railway Warrant to Canterbury.

God Save the King.

On November 10th The Broadstairs & St Peters Mail reported under the headline

LITTLE LEAGUE OF LITTLE HELPERS

We really must accord a word of praise to the ladies of Broadstairs & St Peters for the splendid work they are performing for the local men, either at the Front or prisoners of war in Germany. We like to think of them as the Little League of Little Helpers as we record week by week the activities of the local committees, & we do not believe a local man goes without his parcel of comforts & food, thanks to the way in which the organisation & support of all the Broadstairs & St Peters residents is carried out.

The Little League of Helpers have received many kind messages of thanks from men at the Front.

On November 24th the Mail reported,

So busy have the Little Band of Helpers, (the name stuck), been this month in ensuring all the local serving men will receive their Christmas parcel that they have taken over the premises of the International Stores in Albion Street, Broadstairs. The secretaries have been ably helped by Miss M Bevan & Miss Beasley. Mr Williams, the manager, took unlimited trouble in helping the packers by building a special long counter in the middle of the shop, for preparing all of the boxes, covers & packing materials.

Mr Hemstead, the well know Albion Street confectioner, has been baking special bread to a special recipe for sending to Germany. Fifty six loaves in all have been given to the parcels fund.

Parcels were also being packed at Vyes in St Peters, "Who have put part of the shop at the disposal of the Little League".

Broadstairs Printing & Publishing Co., Ltd.

: **Private Greeting Cards** :

¶ SUITABE WORDS AND DESIGNS ON INEXPENSIVE CARDS WILL BE LOOKED FOR THIS XMAS.

¶ WE HAVE JUST THE RIGHT AND APPROPRIATE THING FOR THE TRENCHES, THE FLEET, OR RELATIVES AT HOME.

17, High Street.

MEN ON **HOME SERVICE** Are also entitled to receive the Xmas Presents now being sent from the town. Relatives should send their addresses in **At Once** to the "Echo" office.

Chairman of the Council.

To most of the early service volunteers, the war had offered an escape. It promised them excitement, adventure & a different way of life, & an opportunity of going abroad, something they could only have dreamed of in the past. Some volunteers joined a regiment going as far away from home as possible, just to receive their first long train journey. Others, particularly the under age, put as many miles as possible between them & their parents in fear of being followed, & that happened on more than one occasion. The dangers were played down, but there was always the possibility of returning as a war hero. The early volunteer was fed with the information "*It will all be over by Christmas*", (1914), but that hadn't proved to be the case. After some of the early campaigns had proved to be disastrous, more men were required & conscription was being called for by the end of 1915.

Lord Derby, the Director General of Recruiting, persuaded the Government to give the volunteer system one last try. His idea was to persuade men to come forward, enlist, but go back to their jobs until they were called. After that, conscription would be brought in.

The Mail reported, "*The news from the fighting Fronts east & west, has made men think. The lads who were in their first flush of youth were quick to answer the call. Many of them lie now in soldiers graves in Flanders or Gallipoli. War to them was to be the beginning of a great adventure. In truth this war which England has not seen yet, save for the streams of wounded returning home, & the lists of those killed*".

Recruiting, once again started in earnest, first in Ramsgate, & Margate, & then in Broadstairs. Those left behind from the earlier recruitment drives were predominantly married men, & what were considered to be shirkers amongst the single men. Shame was first brought upon the latter group, who slowly signed up. Married men were "leaned" on, repeating the atrocities carried out on the Belgian & French women & children, & what would happen if the Germans reached these shores. The murder of Nurse Edith Cavell, was often used as an example of the brutality of the Germans towards women.

Becoming a conscript & being made to fight for one's country was a stigma many married men were not prepared to accept & a rush of volunteers took place before conscription was introduced. The recruitment office at No 19 The Broadway & the Council Offices, which was used as an overspill, were kept busy. On 15th December one of the last recruitment drives of the year took place at Broadstairs, & produced the largest batch of volunteers so far.

LORD DERBY'S SCHEME AT BROADSTAIRS

A GREAT RECRUITING RALLY

WILL TAKE PLACE

IN EAST KENT

ON

Saturday, October 2nd,

AND

Sunday, October 3rd,

IN THE FOLLOWING CENTRES:

Ashford	Margate
Dover	Ramsgate
Folkestone	Sittingbourne

The Towns and Villages in their vicinity will be visited by Military Bands and Troops and addresses will be given by well-known speakers to show

The Urgent Necessity of Every Enlistable Man Joining the Army Now.

GOD SAVE THE KING.

In all the long history of war, there has been nothing to equal the rush of manhood of Broadstairs, St Peters, & neighbouring environs, during the latter days of last week, to offer their services to both King & Country.

The district may well be proud of the response made by men of all ranks & conditions, from the humble working man, to the businessman, presenting themselves for attestation.

Since the scheme was introduced, the flow of recruits has been slow but sure, but the rush over the last few days has been overwhelming.

Every effort has been made for the recruiting staff of the district to deal with the men presenting themselves as expediently as possible, & on Friday extra clerical help was called in to cope with the work. Some voluntary helpers rendered valuable service on Saturday & Sunday, when the recruiting offices were kept open to Midnight.

At 6 pm on Friday evening, there was a long queue in waiting. As fast as one man was dealt with, then another took his place. The same applied on Saturday. On Sunday, the rush slackened off. It was a remarkable culmination of a remarkable week.

We understand that a number of armlets have been issued. Those who are desirous of obtaining same must present their white card at Broadstairs Police Station.

There is a story of one Broadstairs lad who was so desirous of joining the army, he repeatedly offered himself at different recruiting depots. He was a fine specimen of manhood & although not much over seventeen years old, his height was 6ft 2in, & his physique that of a grown man. At each depot he passed the doctors tests easily, but when he gave his age he was dismissed in each case. At last as a forlorn hope he turned into the last recruiting office he could find, & went once more through the process of examination. Asked by the recruiting officer, what was his age, he replied he was just seventeen. The captain eyed the prospective recruit, but expressed a doubt about the question of his age. The Broadstairs lad, like most Broadstairs lads was accustomed in telling the truth, & regretfully told the same answer again. The officer, however expressed even greater doubt than before, & suggested that he should walk round the table until he could remember his **correct** age. At the nineteenth circuit the recruits face lit up with the light of understanding. Today he wears the King's colours.

(Broadstairs & St Peters Echo 1915)

SERGT. A. BENNETT late of the 16th Bedfordshire Regt., has been appointed by the War Office as RECRUITING SERGEANT for Broadstairs.

All young men wishing to join now should report themselves at the

COUNCIL OFFICES,

or

19, THE BROADWAY,

from 12 to 1 p.m., or 5 to 6 p.m.

HONOUR

Englishmen your Honour
Rests with you today
Are you in the Army?
Out amidst the fray
Or are you in the Navy
A sailor clad in blue
Or making shells for soldiers
That's work for English too
Perhaps the doctors termed you
"Medically unfit"
Perhaps you're just a slacker
Afraid to do you're bit
Englishmen, your Honour
Rests with you today
Will you join the Army?
Could you stay away?

Hilda Slade Broadstairs

LADY DRURY'S SPEECH

Several hundred women, the wives & relatives of local men serving at the Front were entertained at the Bohemia on Friday afternoon, & an impressive address was given by Lady Drury, wife of Admiral Drury.

After the singing of the National Anthem, Lady Drury referred to the valuable work the women at home were doing. This war has opened up a great many opportunities for women, & though actually debarred from the actual fighting, they could do their utmost endeavour to overcome evil by doing everything possible at home, & by training their daughters for the inevitable trying times ahead.

During tea time, Mrs Nash kindly gave several pianoforte solos, & some songs were rendered by two ladies present.

Mrs Brightman proposed a vote of thanks to Mrs Drury, which was carried unanimously.

On December 15th, the Post Office at Ramsgate announced that it had enlisted ten women to act as Postwomen in Ramsgate & Broadstairs.

"*Preliminary training is done locally, only taking about a week*".

"*It is certain that now the postwomen have arrived, they will be here to stay*", commented the Mail.

Important.
CHRISTMAS PRESENTS FUND.

¶ The Committee administering this Fund desire to ask that the relatives and friends of all local officers and men serving in the Navy or Army will kindly furnish the full rank, regimental number, and full address of each man, whether at home or abroad. They hope that by this assistance no officer or man will fail to receive a Christmas Gift from his fellow townsmen.

¶ It is also requested that the information be given at the "Echo" office, 17, High Street.

FRANK BRIGHTMAN,
Chairman.

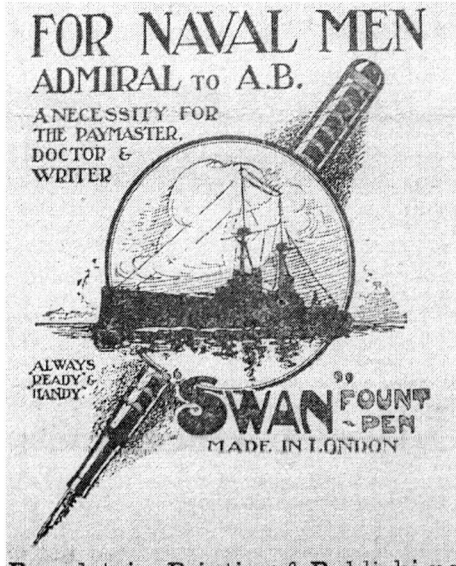

FOR NAVAL MEN
ADMIRAL TO A.B.
A NECESSITY FOR THE PAYMASTER, DOCTOR & WRITER

ALWAYS READY & HANDY

SWAN FOUNTPEN
MADE IN LONDON

Broadstairs Printing & Publishing Company.

On Thursday Nov 11th, the Council sponsored an auction sale at the Bohemia in aid of the Broadstairs Volunteers & Ramsgate Hospital. There were a large number of bidders present, & bidding was very brisk. There were many items of everyday use to be found as in an average sale but the bulk of the goods were antiques or souvenirs. There was a valuable old gold chatelaine with pendants, another was an original Punch sketch done by the Art Editor F H Townsend.

There were four Arundel prints, a set of Maundy Money, a painting on glass by Dudley Forsyth, Belgian exhibition stamps, an autographed letter of Charles Dickens. Autographs of King George III, George IV, William IV, Edward VII, & the Duke of Wellington were also to be had. A generous bidder, Mr Hempstead bid 25/- for a bunny rabbit, offered by a little invalid girl, who had nothing else to give, (she was allowed to keep the rabbit). A pig was given by one gentleman, & a peacock by someone else.

War Relief Committee.
DR. BRIGHTMAN, Chairman.   W. B. URRY, Esq., Treasurer.
Under the patronage of the MAYOR AND MAYORESS OF RAMSGATE.

AN
AUCTION SALE
OF
CURIOS, ANTIQUES,
HOUSEHOLD FURNITURE
Useful & Ornamental Articles, Provisions, Live and Dead Stock, &c.,
IN AID OF THE FUNDS OF THE

BROADSTAIRS   &   **RAMSGATE**
V.A.D.   **HOSPITALS.**

WILL BE HELD AT
Bohemia, High Street, Broadstairs
ON
THURSDAY, NOV. 11th, 1915.

This was purchased by Mr Gullick for 30/- & will now reside at his house The Banks.

The goods had been arriving since Saturday, & were guarded by two Special Constables picked for the event. Goods which were of little intrinsic value fetched far higher prices for their real worth. Three eggs sold for £2, & alongside the homemade cakes & vegetables, found their way to the invalid soldiers at Fairfield. One item was put up for sale fifty three times.

The total raised was £155.

MORE OIL

Whatever shortages exist in Broadstairs there is no little lack of oil. The shores are daily lapped by gentle waves of oil, & a thick dark gummy substance which was once oil. After a walk on the greasy sands, I came to the conclusion that if all other things in life slipped away from us, there would still be sufficient oil to smooth the troubled waves of life in these warring times.

Letter to Editor of Broadstairs & St Peters Echo

Such was the amount of shipping sunk in the channel!

Through all the hardships & difficulties of being at war, local men were still able to find time for poetry. From Driver W H Page of Broadstairs serving with the Army Service Corps, somewhere in France,

THE ARMY SERVICE CORPS

We aren't in the firing line
We are not with the gun
We never do any chasing
When the enemy run,
But when Tommy wants his supper
& we are not to the fore
There's a blooming lot of cussing
At the Army Service Corps.

Our fighting 'aint with bullets
But we are no bally fool
We can drive a traction engine
Or a commissary mule
We've got to get them forward
& all the blooming stores
For its what the, where the, what's up
With the Army Service Corps

When the engines bent its axle
& the trucks have left the tracks
& the whole span of stubborn mules
Are turning on their backs
When the wagons toppled over
& you can't do any more
Its O God of Battle, help us
In the Army Service Corps

We are working in the wharves
We are toiling in the trains
We are boiling in the sunshine
Or dripping in the rains
We are sweating in the storeroom
Or sleeping on the floor
Its eternal marching orders
To the Army Service Corps

There's a lot of decorations
That we never come across
& we've little chance of getting
Near a bronze Victoria Cross
But they'll make some decorations
An' give medals by the score
To the man who'll make the timesheets
For the Army Service Corps.

The following was from Private Haggis of the R A M C who was fighting the Turks with the Mediterranean Forces. Writing to his brother in Broadstairs

THERES A NEAT LITTLE HOME IN TRENCH

There's a neat little home in a trench
Which the rainstorms occasionally drench
There's a dead Turk close by
With his toes to the sky
& he throws off a terrible stench.

The bully & biscuits we chew
Its days since we last had some stew
But with shells bursting there
What place can compare
With my neat little home in a trench.

There are snipers who keep on the go
So you must bob your napper down low
& star shells at night
Make a deuce of a sight
Which causes the language to flow.

Over there is a place on the floor
It's a mass of hard rock & some straw
But with shells bursting there
There's no place to compare
With my neat little home in the trench.

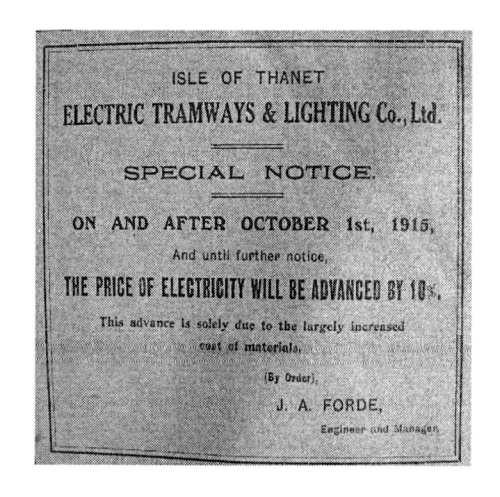

ISLE OF THANET
ELECTRIC TRAMWAYS & LIGHTING Co., Ltd.

SPECIAL NOTICE.

ON AND AFTER OCTOBER 1st, 1915,
And until further notice,
THE PRICE OF ELECTRICITY WILL BE ADVANCED BY 10%.

This advance is solely due to the largely increased cost of materials.

(By Order),
J. A. FORDE,
Engineer and Manager.

Great Annual Sale!
Phone 6x. **H. G. WATSON,** Phone 6x.
Thanet Useful Stores,
ST. PETER'S ROAD AND SOWELL STREET.

Buy at our Sale and help Send Parcels to
Broadstairs & St. Peter's
: Men at the Front. :

1d. in 1/- of every Cash Purchase for the Fund until End of Dec.

Many Special Lines. See Window & Tickets.

THANET USEFUL STORES, Upton Road

35

1916

1916 started off badly locally with the news of the destruction of H.M.S. Natal at Cromarty Firth in Scotland on the 30th December 1915.

H.M.S.NATAL

Many Thanet men were serving on the armoured cruiser which was moored along the quayside. Fire broke out on board which spread to a magazine, the catastrophic explosion destroyed the ship which capsized in five minutes with the loss of 421 officers & men. News filtered through over the next few days that Captain Eric Back of Hartsdown in Margate who was in command lost his life, as did Leading Seaman Jervis of Ramsgate. Another Ramsgate resident, Petty Officer Port was fortunately saved. Sick Berth Steward J.Archibald Jenkins of Shannonville, Dundonald Road, was killed whilst tending the injured. Ordinary Seaman Stanley Drayson of 53 Albion Street was missing, feared drowned. Leading Carpenter Alfred Harty of 57 Albion Street was fortunately on leave at the time of the explosion. Leslie C. Pantony of 1 Camden Villas Green Lane was also safe, as was Ordinary Seamen Edward Stupples of 1 Calva Cottages St Peters.

H M S Natal was built by Vickers in 1905, & was commissioned in 1907, at a cost of £1,218,244. It was 550 feet long with a beam of 73 feet, & armed with six 9.8 inch & four 7.5 inch guns, & underwater torpedo tubes.

On 12th January, a shot was fired in the Droit Office at Broadstairs. The bullet passed through a window, which smashed, & struck a lamp post on the pier.
The Commanding Officer of the Local Volunteer Force explained that the incident was an accident, & apologised to the Council for damaging their property.
Broadstairs & St Peters Mail.

After the recruiting drive of the previous month, rules for medical cases were laid down.
It has been announced that armlets will be issued to the medically unfit from January 15th.
Armlets will be issued to those who have presented themselves for service duty, but are medically unfit. The armlets will be khaki & of the existing army pattern. Those who are medically unfit will be split into two separate classes.
A) Men who are fit owing to an organic disease
B) Men who have a physical defect.
Those in B) will pass into the Army Reserve, & will be called up at any time for immediate service. They will be assessed for suitable work.

Those in A) will not be attested, but their names will be registered. Both classes will return to their normal occupations until ordered otherwise.

New licensing laws also came into being in January. The opening hours were now 12 midday to 2.30, & from 6pm till 8pm throughout the week.

If spirits are required urgently for medical reasons, then the request MUST be accompanied by a signed & dated Doctors certificate.

There was a steady stream of thank you letters from recipients of the Christmas parcels sent to the men on active service. Particularly appreciated was the air pillow, which had been sent to all of the men. A new year letter from Seaman E.J.Wish who was a Prisoner of War at Doeberitz in Germany who wrote to his parents at Blagdon House in Edge End Road,

"*We are all thinking of England & friends who are at home. We consider ourselves well off now with everything we wish for, both to eat & wear, a good wardrobe, & larder, (under the bed). The parcels from Broadstairs are splendid & the bread is much appreciated. It is real xmas weather here, deep snow, & the thick boots & extra clothing are welcome.*

I tip wagon loads of gravel which the others bring out of the mine. We can all do hard work now, & are all well & cheerful".

Sergeant H W Hills wrote from "somewhere in France",

"*Many thanks for the nice parcel received today from the people of Broadstairs. Everything the parcel contained came in beautifully, especially the socks. The chief complaint here is the frost bite, & a clean pair of socks prevents this. I had a very nice Christmas parcel in the trenches which included an air pillow. I am sorry I failed to acknowledge this in my last letter, not knowing any particular person to thank. A most useful present from the warmest of people, thank you. I am the only Broadstairs lad in the battalion left now. Once again, thank you for your great kindness towards us*".

On average, the "Little Band of Helpers" in Broadstairs & St Peters, was still sending 30 parcels a week out to the Front.

On January 26th, the Mail reported, "*The Special Constables in Broadstairs are an all too familiar sight to us all as one takes a stroll around the town after closing time. You can always be sure to meet the men with the white armbands with brass discs attached on their arms. On Wednesday evening at the Council Offices, 130 Specials were sworn in for their twelve months of duty patrolling the town. The officiating Magistrate, Mr E S Goodson, spoke of the good work they were doing, & thanked the men for volunteering, & doing their duty in these hard times. Captain Couradi, their Captain, said that he had 6 men resigning over the last year, but they had since been replaced. He trusted that they would all continue to work together as they had done in the past twelve months*".

The Government issued restrictions to the press, on what could & couldn't be reported. Anything that the Germans were able to make propaganda use out of, was off the record. In depth details of people & places were strictly off limits, & the recommendation was to leave the details to the press releases from the War Office. This made local reporting nonsensical as in the following case.

16th Feb

On Wednesday evening the Secretary of the War Office made the following announcement.

At 3.30 today, two German sea planes were reported approaching the coast of Kent.

A few minutes later the two planes dropped three bombs in a field in the outskirts of Ramsgate, & four near to a school in Broadstairs, three other bombs failed to explode.

No casualties were reported, & the only damage was to some glass.

It has now been ascertained that as a result of these hostilities, the following were injured.

        Two women & one child.

A number of naval & military aircraft ascended to attack the raiders, but no engagement was reported.

The Mail decided to go into a little more depth

37

BOMBS DROPPED ON RAMSGATE & BROADSTAIRS   ONLY AN INCIDENT NOT A SENSATION

Few people were aware of the raid on the towns until sometime later. The sound of firing is not unknown in the area emanating from the big guns firing out at sea. The day was bright & sunny & many people were out on the front of the towns.

The two planes were flying very high & did not venture inland very far. On approaching Dumpton, one plane went in the direction of Ramsgate, & dropped its bombs near to the Jewish Cemetery. A lady passenger in a passing car remarked, "There was nothing approaching alarm, I was just a little bit startled myself". Another lady passing the spot fainted, but soon recovered.

The other seaplane headed towards Broadstairs, & five or six bombs were dropped causing little damage. One bomb dropped on a ladies school & the classroom ceiling dropped in, slightly injuring the pupils at their lessons. Another house in the vicinity was also slightly damaged.

An eyewitness described the hostile aircraft as like two silver birds. The explosion was heard for a distance around. Several bombs dropped into a field without doing any damage. One was even picked up with the safety pin still in place.

The actual locations & people's names were not permitted to be reported under the new press rules.

What happened in Broadstairs was that the two German seaplanes, one a Friedrichshafer FF33e, & the other a Hansa Brandenburg N W separated over Dumpton, & one of them dropped a series of bombs. The school in question was Bartrum Gables Ladies School in Dumpton Park Drive, (now Bradstow School), where Miss Hermione Macheals was injured from falling debris from the ceiling. A maid, Alice Earlop, was also injured.

Another five bombs dropped on "Teneriffe" in Dumpton Park Drive where a Miss Stevens face was cut by flying glass.

Though food was still freely available, the prices were starting to rise alarmingly. Prices in & around the local shops were watched diligently, & with a little shopping around it was usually possible to pick up a bargain or two. Suppliers particularly of fresh vegetables, could see problems looming on the horizon, with so many of the local producers having been called up, but the agriculture industry & the Government had yet to do anything about it.

WHERE THE FOOD IS CHEAPER

Broadstairs traders had an entirely unsolicited testimonial in the "Daily Mail" on Monday.

A correspondent who keeps a house in both Broadstairs & London was comparing commodity prices, & all were in favour of the Thanet town. Meat showed a variation of 4d per pound, & all the meat was killed locally. Eggs were 4d a dozen cheaper, & were fresher as they were collected in the district. Salmon, middle cut must have come from away, but in London the price is half as much again, another saving, this time 11d, by purchasing in Broadstairs.

Loaf sugar, box biscuits, & butter were all imported into the district but the coastal town still had the lower prices.

The problem facing most people is living on a fixed income, although prices are continuously rising.

After much discussion, the Council decided to carry on with the seaside entertainments for the summer season. All the usual sand privileges were put out to tender, apart from the minstrel troupe, Mr Summerson, "Uncle Mack", having already having written to the Council, saying that he had volunteered for the war effort. He would carry on as usual but might be called away at anytime. He was actually called up in October 1916, & so completed the season at Broadstairs.

On March 1st, the first of the military tribunals were held at the Council Officers in Broadstairs. These were to hear the claims for exemption from military service. Many of the claimants were single men claiming exemption on the grounds that they were the sole supporter of a single parent, or were businessmen claiming hardship to their business, *even the curious "bird", the conscientious objector appeared.* The Tribunal consisted of Rev F G Ridgway as the Chairman, Rev W H Churchill, A J Richardson, Harry Bing, H T Gullick of the Local Volunteer Force, Dr F Brightman, Mr E E Moody, Mr W H Shrew, with the Military representatives Mr L A Skinner, & Mr F E Hill.

The first case was that of a farmer who asked for absolute exemption on the grounds that though the farm was in his father's name, he had absolutely nothing to do with farming. All of his farmhands had joined up, leaving him & his wife to run the farm alone. Exemption was granted.

Another young man asked for exemption as he had a bedridden mother to support. Two of his brothers were fighting, leaving just him & his sister to care for her. The Tribunal said that she would be no worse off if he joined up, as his mother would get her full allowances. The case was dismissed.

A Broadstairs tradesman, who specialised in "difficult work", applied for absolute exemption on the grounds of serious hardship if he was to serve. Applicant said that he had invested all his money in his business & his shop was on a 21 year lease. He had been unable to find a suitable replacement. A fortnight's exemption was allowed, before he was to report for call up.

The first case of a conscientious objector was next. The applicant was an insurance agent whose plea that his allegiance to Christ prevented him from undertaking military service. He was a member of the Christadelphinians who forbade such things. The Chairman asked, *"If your father or mother were attacked by a German, would you defend them"?* *"If I did kill a man my conscience would be in a terrible condition"*, was the reply. *"I object to non-combatant service".* *"On what grounds"*, asked the chairman. There was no reply. The Chairman then asked, *"you are not prepared to pay attention to military officers is that correct".* *"Yes".* The Chairman, *"Do you pay income tax"? "No".* Asked if he objected to minesweeping, the applicant said he did. Dr Brightman then asked, *"Are you going to live in this country when the war is over"? "Yes"* was the reply. The applicant was ordered to do non-combatant service & join up immediately.

A 39 year old market gardener was next, & claimed exemption on the grounds that he was the only one left. *"Exemption denied"*, announced the Chairman.

A 19 year old conscientious objector describing himself as a sorting clerk & telegraphist applied for absolute exemption. The applicant said that he was a Plymouth Brethren which is apposed to all forms of military service. After much questioning by the Tribunal, he said that if he saw a woman in danger, he would not feel justified in committing a crime to save her. He would let her die if need be, & pray for her soul. *"Germany"*, he said, *" would not invade this country if all the people humbled themselves before God".* *"What about the people of Belgium, did they humble themselves before God"?* asked the Chairman. There was no reply. The military representative of the Tribunal said the applicant had stated his reasons, which weren't good enough, & he would be put into the Royal Engineers Post Office, delivering mail.

The next applicant was a farmer on behalf of a horseman aged 21 who worked for him. The employer said that if the man went, he would not be able to keep his remaining men employed. Dr Brightman said that he had employed women in 1915, were they that unsuccessful? *"Yes"*, was the reply. One month's exemption was granted.

A 33 year old builder & decorator claimed that had several contracts to finish which would depend on the weather & his labour, & if unfinished he would suffer financial hardship. The application was refused.

A young man of 22 whose occupation he described as professional stated that he supported his invalid sister & aged mother. His father was very ill in London. On being pressurised by the Tribunal, the man finally admitted that he had never worked, his mother was living in furnished accommodation, & his father worked in a London beer house. *"Application refused, enlists at once"*, was the verdict.

It took a further three sessions that week before the Tribunal got through the first batch of applications.

A letter was published in the Broadstairs & St Peters Mail on the 16th March from a "Broadstairs Tommy" with the Expeditionary Force in France. *"I hope you will forgive me for intruding on your valuable paper, but I was surprised to read in a recent issue of the Mail, that we have men in Broadstairs, who owing to a certain creed to which they belong, they are not allowed to take up arms. May I say that they should all be non-combatants, & they should be the men to put up the barbed wire entanglements on the front line of the trenches. If they still had a conscience, it would be then, as they would be in no doubt by that time, realise WHAT they were fighting for. They would be fighting for King & country & for those that they love, & to save the motherland from pillage & destruction like Belgium & France.*

Come on men of Broadstairs, roll up with a good heart, & let's finish the job".

URBAN DISTRICT OF BROADSTAIRS AND ST. PETER'S.

CANADIAN FUND.

APPLICATIONS are invited from Boarding-house and Lodging-house keepers who desire to participate in the above Fund so generously provided by the Canadian Government. Only those who have not sufficient means to enable them, without assistance, to pay their rent or mortgage interest need apply. For the present the Fund will be distributed subject to the conditions following :
(1) The grant is to be used only for the assistance of Boarding-house and Lodging-house keepers.
(2) The grant is to be confined to the payment of Rent and Interest on Mortgages.
(3) The grant is only available where the landlord agrees to forego part of the rent or interest, as the case may be.
(4) In any individual case the grant must not exceed £30.
(5) Assistance under the scheme is to be restricted to Boarding-house and Lodging-house Keepers who, but for the war, would have been solvent, and who may be regarded as having a reasonable prospect of a return to independence after the war.

Application must be made on a form which can be obtained from the undersigned.

L. A. SKINNER,
Hon. Secretary to the Fund.
Council Offices, Broadstairs.
May 30th, 1916.

Owing to the war, the Council elections were postponed again in 1916. Dr Brightman was re-elected as Chairman, & the various committees continued unchanged. Thanking them for their renewed confidence in him, Dr Brightman said, *He would be pleased to be their Chairman once again, & hoped that by the end of the year the war would be over, & they could return to some resemblance of order. He mentioned that they must continue as best they can, but they must follow the policy of strict economy. He thought he should publicly acknowledge the handsome donation of £1,100 from the Canadian Society, which had practically all been used up. This was used to help the suffering from the effects of war, in helping to pay their rents.*

He went on to say that Broadstairs rates have dropped in the last year from 4s 1d to 3s 2d. The Council Surveyor had done recent routine inspections of the billets in the town, & had requested certain improvements to sanitary arrangements where necessary. These landladies were getting 6d per man per night, & the least we can do is to make sure we keep the standards as high as they were before the war.

Once again they had written to the War Office requesting more troops to be billeted in the town, but had received no replies. They were after another 1,000 men, which would do the town a lot of good. Letters were becoming a waste of time, & it was thought that a deputation should be organised.

SUCCESSFUL CONCERT AT BROADSTAIRS, March 1st

A successful concert was held at the Cinema in the High Street on Wednesday evening. The concert was arranged by the Fife & Drum Band of the Broadstairs Company of the Kent Volunteer Fencibles, the proceeds were in aid of the Band Equipment Fund.

Great credit is due to Sergeant Drummer Griffiths for the way in which the Band rendered various selections, as the Band has only been formed a short time. Private Mason, who is becoming quite a local favourite, kept the audience in continual humour

The assembly had an introduction to the eminent artist, Mr Louis Wain, he pleasing them with some lightening sketches, & of course, our old friend the domestic cat predominated. Mr Wain has kindly given his sketches to help swell the funds of the Band. The highest bidder secures the sketches.

THE "GROCERETTE"
The lady grocer's assistant has been dubbed the "grocerette" & our contributor Mr Walter Johnson of Reading Street sends us the following.

The morning is fine, or perchance it is wet
But that does not deter the sweet "grocerette",
As for orders she toddles, with pencil & book,
To wait on our patrons, or chat with the cook.

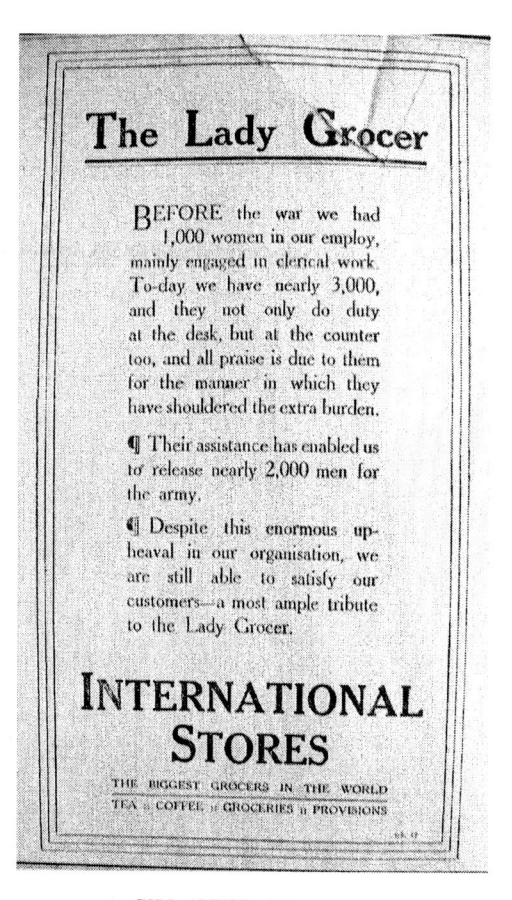

The Lady Grocer

BEFORE the war we had 1,000 women in our employ, mainly engaged in clerical work. To-day we have nearly 3,000, and they not only do duty at the desk, but at the counter too, and all praise is due to them for the manner in which they have shouldered the extra burden.

¶ Their assistance has enabled us to release nearly 2,000 men for the army.

¶ Despite this enormous upheaval in our organisation, we are still able to satisfy our customers—a most ample tribute to the Lady Grocer.

INTERNATIONAL STORES

THE BIGGEST GROCERS IN THE WORLD
TEA :: COFFEE :: GROCERIES :: PROVISIONS

INTERNATIONAL STORES

Nearly **2000** of our men are in the Army, but we have an able and willing staff of lady grocers ready to attend to you.

THE BIGGEST GROCERS IN THE WORLD.
Tea, Coffee, Groceries, Provisions etc.

GIRL ARTIST- REMARKABLE AIR RAID SKETCHES
    Miss Dorothy Hardy, the 15 year old daughter of Mr & Mrs Hardy of the London County & Westminster Bank in the High Street, has completed a collection of coloured sketches, illustrating her impressions of an aeroplane raid recently on our town. This drew special attention at the Royal Drawing Society at the Guildhall in London.
    Miss Hardy's sketches attracted much attention & reproductions of her sketches appeared in several London illustrated papers. The sketches are unique for their colour, humour, accuracy, & skill & are quite remarkable.
    The sketches illustrate in a humorous style a recent air raid where a school was struck by a bomb. These views show a bomb dropping into one of the rooms, the children running downstairs, & watching the

machines depart. In the last view the girls are curiously examining the hole made by the bomb. The drawing makes a special point of the insouciance with which the raiders are regarded by the schoolgirls.

Broadstairs & St Peters Mail April 19th

A KHAKI EASTER AT BROADSTAIRS

Easter passed off rather quietly at Broadstairs, but the most hopeful optimist must have been surprised to see so many people down for their Easter holidays.

The weather was fairly fine throughout the week, so that the outdoor band performances at the bandstand were well patronised. The Sunday evening concert at the cinema by the band of the Rifle Brigade was very well attended, & Mr Newman Wilks, a baritone of some repute, was heard to advantage. The sands on Monday possessed the unmistakable sight of juvenile activity. Right across the stretch of the main bay one could see hundreds of children busy with their spades & pails, & one would imagine their thoughts were absolutely outside the war, were it not for the fact that they employed themselves digging trenches & making parapets in the sand.

The Easter differed from last year inasmuch as there was more khaki in evidence. There were soldiers everywhere; in fact the major proportion of the male population was wearing the King's uniform. Not only were khaki uniforms present but the ladies favoured the colour in their dresses. We can safely say that the Easter results exceeded expectations, indeed anyone requiring a wartime holiday need have no fear of selecting Broadstairs. The town's affairs are in capable hands & whilst it is futile to expect the same boom as in pre-war years, it is safe to say that the coming season should come up to war time expectations.

On the Thursday evening the "Granville Express" left at Broadstairs, a compliment of visitors which surprised more than one local man. A railway official also emphasised the view, "Yes Broadstairs has got some visitors, even though the cheaper fares were unavailable, they cannot forget our little place at Easter during this war".

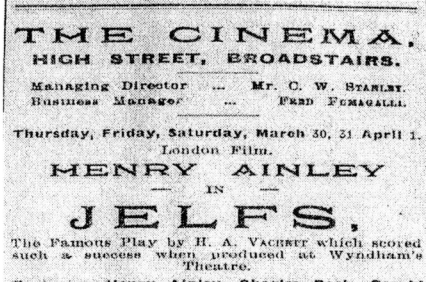

The news of the sinking of H M S Russell on 26th April was received with gloom & apprehension in Broadstairs. The Duncan class battleship H M S Russell hit two mines laid by the German submarine U73, in the Mediterranean off the coast of Malta. 125 members of the crew were lost but fortunately 625 men were rescued. It finally filtered through that all the local men serving on board were amongst the survivors.

"Safe & well", was the message received by telegram from Ordinary Seaman W T Sears to his parents at 37 Queens Road. Mr Sears worked for Kelsys the bakers in the High Street before the war. Petty Officer John Murphy of "Rosemary" in Beacon Road was also saved. Although not on board at the time, having been just transferred to torpedo boats, 1st Class Stoker Harry Shersby also informed his parents at 1 Upton Cottage that he was safe & well. Petty Officer W A Southern of 27 Church Street also sent a telegram to his parents. Three Margate men were also amongst the survivors.

Broadstairs & St Peters Mail May 3rd

Just to make the troops feel at home, the Cinema was showing *"The Making of an Officer"*, with the British Army in France.

COMPULSION FOR ALL May 3rd,

The Prime Minister has laid before Parliament an updated Military Service Bill. The scheme was outlined as
1 Bring into Military Service all youths under 18 years on August 15th last, as they reach that age
2 Make unattested men up to 41 years liable to serve
3 Remaining time served men until the end of the war
4 Allow Territorials to be transferred to other units as the Military see fit
5 Make exempted men liable to serve, immediately to serve when their exemption certificates expire.
The Government will meet the needs of hardship under the Military Tribunal Scheme.
Assistance will be given in regard to rent, mortgage interest, payments of instalments in virtue of contracts, taxes, insurance premiums & school fees.
The assistance in any one case not to exceed £104 per annum.

On May 10th over 120 Emergency Special Constables were sworn in at the Council Offices on Friday evening before Magistrates. Messrs G K Binge J P & E S Goodson J P. The oath was taken en-bloc by the volunteers. Mr H Hicks, head Special Constable for the area, outlined the nature of their duties & each man was served with his warrant.

It should be noted that the Emergency Specials are an entirely separate body from the Special Constables already in existence in the town, & were not liable to patrol duties. Only in case of an emergency would they be required.

There was another air raid over Broadstairs on the night of the 19th & 20th May. This was once again not reported in the local paper, though it was the biggest raid of the war so far. Seven enemy aircraft approached the town from the Kingsgate direction, & dropped bombs in the field by Whitfield Tower, the Tram Depot in Northdown Road, Rumfields Water Tower, & at Bromstone Farm. Apparently the only casualties were some chickens at the farm.

The aircraft then did more damage at Ramsgate before moving on down the coast to Deal & Dover.

On Sunday May 24th, there was a successful egg collection in aid of the wounded at Roseneath & Fairfield V A D Hospitals. The work was undertaken by the Misses Daniel & Evelyn. Children were asked to bring eggs to church with them, & 287 eggs were collected from the churches around the town, & 89 at Sunday Schools, making a total of 376 eggs collected on the day.

Also on May 24th, the clock on Reading Street refused to acknowledge the Daylight Saving Bill. Although all of the other public clocks in Broadstairs were put forward one hour on Sunday, this clock was evidently forgotten, & on Monday was still registering the old time.

QUALIFIED FIREMEN WANTED for H.M. YACHT PATROL.
Employed on Active Service.

CONDITIONS OF SERVICE.—Sign on for period of the War for service in any yacht. No Separation Allowance, but men may make weekly allotments from their pay to dependants.

PAY.—30/- per week, with an addition of 10/- food allowance. Suitable men are selected for Greasers, with total pay of 43/- per week.

CLOTHING GRATUITY of £6.

During May the Government reduced the imports of wood & paper pulp. This created a shortage of paper, & consequently increased its price. All newspapers were limited to what was available, & it was imperative that wastage was reduced to a minimum. Unsold newspapers were to be eliminated, & all papers, including those previously "free" to hospitals, various institutions, libraries & clubs, had to be paid for. All advertisements were to be limited.

On the 31st May the Parish Hall of St Andrews Church was opened for the use of the troops. Evening sessions were from 6 to 9pm, with all kinds of entertainment, card games, reading materials being provided.

Another 32 parcels were despatched to the Front by the "Little League" this week. The "Little League" acknowledges with thanks the most useful present of "bachelors buttons" from Mrs Smith which were included in the parcels. The "Little League" could do with a great many more subscribers of from 2d to 1/- a week. The funds are rather like the "widows curse". They have never quite failed to cover expenses, but they generally need very careful nursing in spite of occasional windfalls. In future all addresses should be sent to Mrs H Raven of Barfield House, who also has the wool for the knitting of socks etc.

The "Little League" is sorry to hear that Mrs Goold is leaving the town, & wish her all the success in her canteen work at Woolwich. The parcel system that is now well known was originally started by Mrs Goold & Mrs Vines, & the success of the undertaking is due to Mrs Goold's good work & enthusiasm.

(Personal additions to parcels up to 3lb in weight go free, over that the charge is 4d.)

W. P. BLACKBURN & SON,
Linoleum, Carpet & Curtain Factors.

Notwithstanding the general shortage of raw materials and labour, we have purchased large new stocks of Linoleums, Carpets and Curtains from the best BRITISH MANUFACTURERS and our prices will compare favourably with the prices ruling in London Markets.

69, 71 & 73, King Street, Ramsgate,
PHONE 9x.
And at YORK STREET, BROADSTAIRS,
PHONE 30.

The Council's Pier & Harbour accounts from March 1915 to 31st March 1916 showed an expenditure of £803.13.8d, & an income of £1,696.17.11d, making a gross profit of £893.4.2d.

CENSORSHIP 7th June

The Council at their meeting on Monday agreed with the proposals contained in a letter from the Secretary of State in regard to the censorship of cinematic films. In the circular it was stated that a number of Chief Constables had expressed an opinion that a good deal of the juvenile delinquency that is now rife, was due to the objectionable films being shown, & the Secretary of State's solution was that an establishment, by the Government, of a central & independent form of censorship would be set up.

Broadstairs & St Peters Mail

THE CALL 11th June

This week the last of the Derby Groups, (last Decembers volunteers), were called up, & we have, for the first time in England, the whole of the manhood of the Country in arms. Everyman fit to serve is in uniform, or should be. The nation now realises that every ounce of our strength must be thrown into the scale if we are to win through. Men have made sacrifices cheerfully, knowing that we are in a life or death struggle. It is not the time to weigh individual losses against our duty as a nation.

Editor, Broadstairs & St Peters Mail.

Mr J Richmond who was on holiday from Camden Square in London, wrote, *"There is some confusion as to the use of glasses,* (telescopes & binoculars), *on the coast at Broadstairs. Last week I was challenged, whilst looking out to sea, by a military officer, for using a pair of white opera glasses.*

He informed me that I had no right to a glass within one mile of the sea, & added that it was his duty to confiscate them, & take me & them to Broadstairs Police Station. Many residents are obviously unaware of this rule, as the uses of glasses were in general use, as any observer could see".

On taking up the challenge the Editor of the Mail, found that the rule had been rescinded earlier in the year as being unnecessary, which led to the council reinstating the telescope concession back on the seafront?

Collections were still being carried out throughout the town for anything that could be useful, either on its own, or traded for money to raise funds for the various soldiers & sailor's charitable funds

A scheme is afoot in Broadstairs for the regular collection of old bottles & jam jars. These will be sold to support the work of the "Little League" in sending parcels to the Front. Mr Stillman of the "York

Gate Fruit Stall" in Albion Street, (next to the Dolphin Public House), will receive all such articles & dispose of them.

Another venture started in July was collection of surplus fruit & vegetables. This was to go to the minesweepers that were permanently patrolling the channel off the Kent coast. This was once again organised by Mrs Raven of Barfield House in Albion Street. (No doubt with Mr Stillman's help)! On August 2nd the Mail reported,

MINESWEEPERS APPRECIATION

There has been a fair supply of fruit & vegetables for the minesweepers again this week, & though a sack full can not go very far between 100 men, very grateful letters have been received. One from Lieutenant H W Noakes R N V R , "I wish to thank you on behalf of my crew & that of the other sweepers in my section for the vegetables that you have sent on board yesterday. These have been distributed amongst the vessels in my section. Please accept my assurance that your kindness has been appreciated & I have had signals from all my ships asking me to thank you. My vessel was so close this morning that the distribution of the vegetables could be quite clearly be seen with glasses. It took place immediately after the rush for newspapers.

On August the 23rd the organisation of the Yarrow Hospital in Ramsgate Road was being changed, but no one in the town could work out why.

THE YARROW CHANGE - PUZZLED AUTHORITIES

Since the building was converted from a children's convalescent home into a military hospital in November 1914, a very excellent work has been done. The intimation in connection with the change forwarded to us by the Matron is appended.

"Since November 1914, The Yarrow has been used as a general military hospital under the management committee of the home. During this period over 1,000 wounded men have been treated & many serious operations have been performed.

Sir Arthur Yarrow & his committee have now consented to lend the hospital to the Canadian Authorities & it will be managed by them for the remainder of the war. All communications with the existing hospital should be addressed to Dr G Moon "The Dene", Broadstairs from the 1st of September. The committee desire to take this opportunity in thanking those kind friends who have helped in so many ways to aid & comfort the sick & wounded, & have hastened the recovery, in so many ways. The treatment of patients was under the resident doctor, the Matron, Miss Chambers, & a staff of trained nurses. The Rev C S G Ridgeway acted as Chaplain.

The present patients will all be transferred to other Thanet hospitals for the continuation of their treatment.

Valuable assistance has been rendered locally in transporting the men from the railway station to the hospital. In this direction, the work of Mr Dixon, of the garage in Belvedere Road has proved invaluable.

In the early stages of the war, his efforts to train others in the art of stretcher bearing were of a strenuous character, & using his garage as a "drill ground", were able to give valuable instructions. With the aid of the cars & carts being converted to ambulances, with which the building was soon filled, he speedily became the local controlling spirit of an excellent band of helpers, a fact that numerous soldiers can testify.

He found drivers for the cars lent by generous residents & visitors, & on every occasion on which convoys of the wounded arrived in the district, the removal from stations was carried out with utmost dispatch & care. A simple phone call or message was all it took to get an organised transport system for the wounded, both into & out of the town, set in operation at a minutes notice.

Amongst the gentlemen who did duty at The Yarrow as day & night shift orderlies & acted as stretcher bearers, we give thanks to the following.

Messrs H Blackburn, F Blackburn, A Blackburn, Brett, Beach, H Bing, Bowie, E O Britton, F Coyler, W Cantwell, T Clare, Day, Dixon, F Fumagalli, G Fuggle, Gill, Goodall, Hook, Hall, Hiscote,

Harrington, Hodges, Hoskins, Hicks, A Jarrett, Lewis, Lowlings, Landsdowne, Lawn, W L Nash, Nation, Pettman, Rutland, Strevens, Sutton, Smith, Russell, Reader, F White".

On August 30th
The Telegraph Messenger girls on the staff of Broadstairs Post Office, made their appearance in uniform today.

The "Little League" of helpers have just dispatched their 1,699th parcel to Broadstairs & St Peters soldiers & sailors since they started out in the Autumn of 1914.

The latest Flag Day on Saturday will be for a coal supply for the poor people of Broadstairs & St Peters.
A total of £65.12.11d was raised throughout the district. This enabled the Coal Committee to sell coal to the poor at 1s 6d per hundredweight from October onwards.

WAR SHRINES, (October 4th)

On Tuesday evening, (3rd), the dedication of three wayside shrines took place in St Peters. These were at Magdala Road, Church Street & Beacon Road. This brings the number up to five, the other two being at Sowell Street & Albion Street in Broadstairs.
Writing in the Parish Magazine, the Vicar says, "I want to say first how glad I am to find how many there are taking up the idea of these little war shrines. It makes me wish that we had embarked on the idea some time before. I cannot help the feeling that anything which helps to bring home to us the thought of what our boys are doing for their country. Anything that serves to remind us that they need our prayers, anything that keeps fresh in the memory of those who have laid down their lives for this country, & reminds us that they are still one with us. I am glad that so many have these natural feelings. It is part of the business of the church to help people to find a means of expressing their truest & deepest feelings of their hearts, & these little shrines in our streets will do just that".

The war shrines started appearing in Broadstairs in May of 1916, a consisted of a simple memorial tribute in the form of a wooden cross & a vase of flowers & perhaps a photograph. Other photographs of the fallen & flowers were added as time went on. By the end of the year they were becoming quite elaborate. The Government had declared back at the end of 1914, that the fallen soldiers' & sailors' bodies would not be brought home, though some parents tried at any cost People required somewhere local to mourn their loved ones. Further shrines, one at Reading Street, & another at George Hill were dedicated on October 11th. The Vicar of St Andrews Church in Reading Street removed the two wayside shrines into the church, & specifically fitted out part of the chapel for the purpose. Two more wayside shrines appeared shortly afterwards.
The Vicar of St Peters opened up the "old vestry", to be used as a dedicated war chapel, but the wayside shrines still remained.

At the Military Tribunal on October 11th, the subject of the tramway company employees was put forward by Mr Forde, the manager of the company. He pointed out that his staff had been considerably reduced with the war, & from a staff of 270 on July 1914 he was down to 114 staff including the women & boys he was now employing. If he took the numbers any lower, it would considerably affect the company's undertaking, both in meeting the requirements of the tram operation & the electricity supplies.
He applied for exemption from war duty for two inspectors, who also undertook the driving of tramcars, one storekeeper, the steam engine driver, seven tram drivers, four men who were in charge of the sub-stations, three of whom were all single men. Since the start of the war, he had compelled all of his men to drive the trams where necessary, & all work extended hours to maintain the 15 minute service as directed in his contract.
The Tribunal Chairman asked, "*Could women not be employed as drivers as in other parts of the country*"? Mr Forde replied, "*The Thanet Tramway Company was different to others in the fact that there were so many hills, & it would be impossible to train women to do the work. The Board of Trade would not

sanction it in Thanet". He was quite prepared to withdraw the applications if the military were able to provide substitutes.

After much deliberation, the Tribunal decided that four drivers would be granted conditional exemption, two were refused, & one was granted three months exemption. Both inspectors were exempted on safety grounds, & six months exemption was given to the storekeeper. Three of the sub-station men were granted three months exemption, one a conditional exemption. The steam engine driver also secured conditional exemption. All of the conditions were that the men must stay in the employ of the company, & they were to join the Local Volunteer Reserve, the Special Constables, or the Ambulance Corps.

Others requesting exemption from war duties, although most were in some form of volunteer group, were shopkeepers in the town. Most were in fear of loosing their livelihoods, bankruptcy, & in so doing, loose the roofs over their dependents heads. The Tribunal were sympathetic in most cases, but were being pressurised by the Military Authorities for more men. Though between 600 & 700 men from Broadstairs were serving the colours, the Government still wanted more to step forward. Appeals from tradesmen were regularly turned down at the Central Tribunal at Canterbury.

Dr Brightman & Mr Harry Bing, who sat on the Broadstairs Tribunal & were both town Councillors, thought they could come up with a scheme to support the businessmen of the town. Many bankruptcies had already taken place & it was in the town's interest that it didn't get any worse. After a meeting of one man businesses at the Council Offices on December 31st, a committee of five people was formed to look after the detail. On the committee were Dr Brightman, Mr H J Gullick, Mr J H Skinner, Mr T Piggott, & Mr R J Sprattling. The idea was a scheme to allow one shopkeeper of a similar trade, from a different location in the town to run two shops, in so doing releas the other shopkeeper for war work. *"After all"*, said Dr Brightman, *"basically all it is, is buying items & selling them at a reasonable overhead to keep you in business. The selling part cannot be too hard if the prices are already set, it is not necessary to be competitive just to stay in business, only to make a large profit, & that shouldn't happen in wartime. The buying of stock might be a bit more difficult, but if a shopkeeper was to order for two shops instead of one, it could be beneficial to both of them. All it required was organising"*.

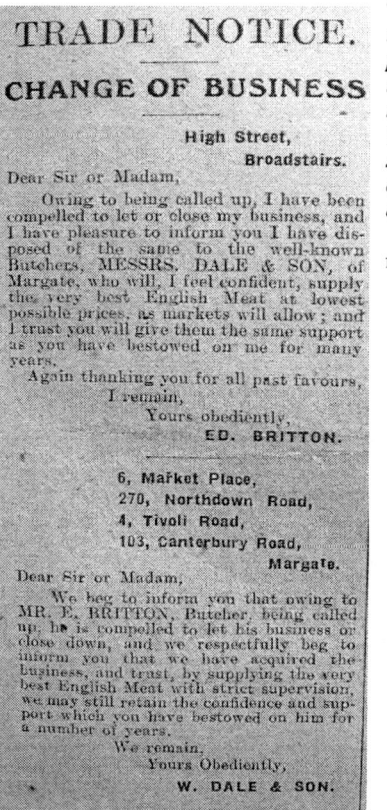

The starting point was an Advisory Board, where men who had been called up could go for advice. By putting

---

TRADE NOTICE.

CHANGE OF BUSINESS

High Street,
Broadstairs.

Dear Sir or Madam,

Owing to being called up, I have been compelled to let or close my business, and I have pleasure to inform you I have disposed of the same to the well-known Butchers, MESSRS. DALE & SON, of Margate, who will, I feel confident, supply the very best English Meat at lowest possible prices, as markets will allow; and I trust you will give them the same support as you have bestowed on me for many years.

Again thanking you for all past favours,
I remain,
Yours obediently,
ED. BRITTON.

6, Market Place,
270, Northdown Road,
4, Tivoli Road,
103, Canterbury Road,
Margate.

Dear Sir or Madam,

We beg to inform you that owing to MR. E. BRITTON, Butcher, being called up, he is compelled to let his business or close down, and we respectfully beg to inform you that we have acquired the business, and trust, by supplying the very best English Meat with strict supervision, we may still retain the confidence and support which you have bestowed on him for a number of years.

We remain,
Yours Obediently,
W. DALE & SON.

PUBLIC NOTICE.

MRS. S. FOWLER

Begs to inform the inhabitants of Broadstairs and St. Peter's that she has acquired the business of her son, F. W. FOWLER, Fruiterer and Greengrocer, and who is now serving with the Colours, and trusts by supplying fresh vegetables and best fruit, with personal supervision, that she may retain the support extended to her son during the past eleven years.

FOWLER'S STORES,
ST. PETER'S ROAD,
BROADSTAIRS.

men of similar trades in contact with one another, & talking round the problems, & the board trying to gain Government grants for rents etc, & writing up a list of agreeable rules, it was thought more men could be released, & their business should survive for them to come back to. Mr J T May, the local builder & also a Councillor, thought the idea was *"utterly ridiculous & would never work"*.

This was a radical first for Broadstairs, & if successful the "Mail" suggested Ramsgate & Margate be advised to copy the idea.

In October there was a letter published in the "Mail" from a member of the Kent County Constabulary, who was stationed in Broadstairs before the outbreak of the war. *"I want to thank you for the parcel received today. The contents arrived in splendid condition, considering the distance that it had travelled. I was only stationed in Broadstairs from 1911 to 1914 as a Police Constable, & it cheers me to think that the same good spirits & wishes exist that were always shown to me in those days. I receive a copy of the "Mail" from an old friend, so am able to read what splendid work you are all doing. A letter or a card from dear old England is better than a tonic. Meal times are nothing compared to "Mail" time. I would like to give you a more detailed account of our work here in Mesopotamia, but Mr Censor wouldn't allow it. We will be thankful when the cooler weather appears"*.

Private R J Bowen of the Royal West Kents wrote from the Western Front, *"Thank you for the parcel packed by you. I should like you thank the "little league" for me. No one can estimate the value of such a parcel out here, until they have been out here in the trenches. It appears that your parcel arrived at base camp as I left for the trenches. I found it very strange & very noisy here for the first day or so, but it is surprising what you get used to. Some of us have been working up to our knees in water & mud in the trenches, & you can guess we did not feel very cheerful, but when we got back to the dugout, the parcels & letters had arrived. We soon forgot out troubles & wet clothes, in fact we forgot the whole ……….. war"*.

The Cinema, High Street, Broadstairs.

THE GREATEST FILM OF ALL TIME

THE BATTLE of the SOMME

THE BIG PUSH.   5,000 FEET IN LENGTH.

Thursday, Friday & Saturday, Sept. 21st, 22nd & 23rd.

Three Exhibitions DAILY, 2.45, 6.30, 8.40.

SEATS CAN NOW BE BOOKED.   Box Office open 10-12.   6.30-10.30.

SHOWN AT WINDSOR CASTLE BY ROYAL COMMAND

H.M. THE KING says:— "The Public should see these pictures that they may have some idea of what the Army is doing and what War means."

H.M. THE QUEEN declared that the pictures were wonderful.

Another enterprising collection fund was started in November, with the aim of raising sufficient money to send a Christmas present to every serving man.

THE 2000 SHILLING FUND, PURSES OPENED IN BROADSTAIRS

That the residents of Broadstairs & St Peters do not intend to forget our lads who are away fighting our battles at Christmas, is apparent from an appeal made by the Chairman of the Council, Dr F Brightman, & Captain Charles Gladstone R N for the provision of Christmas comforts. The objective is to raise a total of 2000 shillings in as short a time as possible.

We have pleasure in responding that between last Wednesday, the start of the appeal, & midday Monday, no less than 665 shillings were subscribed, practically a third of the total. The fund is to give every soldier & sailor serving from the town a Christmas present.

By the following Wednesday the fund had risen too 1238 ½ shillings, (£61.18.6d), or two thirds of the total. Dr Brightman said that the gift will take the form of a collapsible drinking cup, & cigarettes, which will be accompanied by a Christmas card in the form of an almanac. By the following week, (November 15th), 1493 shillings, (£74.13.0d), & on November 22nd, 1558 ½ shillings, (£77.18.6d), had been donated & the appeal was closed.

On November 8th, the Officer Commanding of "D" Battery wrote to the Council saying that he understood that they had two public baths available in Broadstairs, & asked the Council for permission to use same. (these were behind the Council Offices at the Broadway)

Captain C Reed, of the Kent Volunteer Force, thanked the Council for the privilege afforded to the Volunteer Force for drilling at the Bohemia, & asked permission to remove certain seats & make additional arrangements to the lighting. One of the Councillors pointed out that it was impossible to remove the seats as they were all bolted to the floor. Permission was refused.

Also on the 8th November the "Mail" reported

With the changes now effected at the Yarrow Home, a pleasing recognition of the labours of the voluntary Red Cross workers has been made by Sir Alfred Yarrow.

To all those who have assisted at the Yarrow Hospital, he has presented a bronze medal. It consists of a laurel wreath enclosing a shield, & suspended on a red & white ribband. In the shield is inscribed, "Yarrow Military Hospital 1914 - 1916". On the obverse is the recipients name & the words, "In recognition of his sympathetic work to wounded soldiers".

The work at the Yarrow Hospital is now nearing completion, (November 15th), on its conversion to the Canadian Military Hospital. N C O's have been converting the hospital & their labour will be terminated this week when the building will be fully equipped & will give a similar type of treatment to men, partially broken in the war, as at its parent institution at the Granville Canadian Special Hospital at Ramsgate. Two hundred men will be accommodated at the Yarrow, including the personnel. In charge of the treatment will be Lieutenant & Quartermaster J Haylett, as acting Adjutant, & patients will be attended by Captains Beggs & Kenny. The first consignment of patients will arrive this week.

On November 29th the opening of a Y M C A hut in Broadstairs, which was the 52nd to be opened in the S E District, took place.

The local gas company, (in Albion Street), have kindly placed one of its washhouses, free of cost, to the Association,

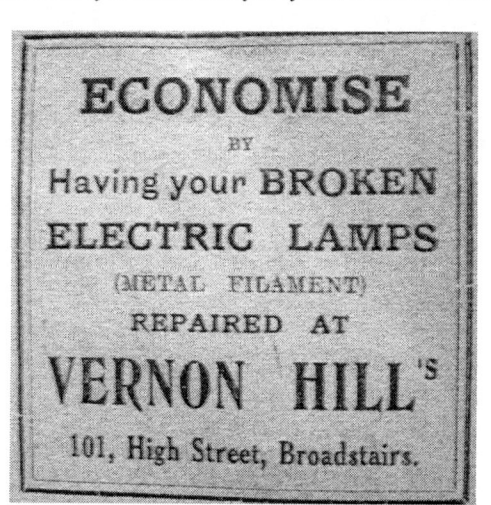

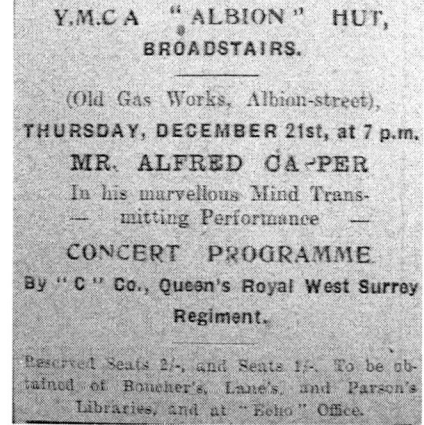

Y.M.C.A "ALBION" HUT, BROADSTAIRS.

(Old Gas Works, Albion-street).

THURSDAY, DECEMBER 21st, at 7 p.m.

MR. ALFRED CASPER

In his marvellous Mind Transmitting Performance

CONCERT PROGRAMME

By "C" Co., Queen's Royal West Surrey Regiment.

Reserved Seats 2/-, and Seats 1/-. To be obtained of Boucher's, Lane's, and Parson's Libraries, and at "Echo" Office.

which has been converted into a cosy room. The hut will consist of a dry canteen, library, & recreation room, & everything that the off duty soldier needs. The hut will be open for the whole of the day, & wounded soldiers will be welcome. The entrance will be from Albion Street.

ECONOMISE
BY
Having your BROKEN ELECTRIC LAMPS
(METAL FILAMENT)
REPAIRED AT
VERNON HILL'S
101, High Street, Broadstairs.

49

Parcels to Prisoners of War for Christmas delivery must be packed by November 14th. Gifts of a personal nature can be put in the prisoners' boxes in many of the shops or at Barfield House. The committee have said that it is intended to send every man a plum pudding as they travel quite well if they are thoroughly boiled. They should be taken out of their basins & allowed to stand for two or three days to allow the steam to thoroughly evaporate. They should then be tied again in the cloth. DO NOT INCLUDE THE BASIN. They must be sufficiently boiled to be eaten cold on arrival, as some of the men have little cooking arrangements.

Mrs Wish of Edge End Road has kindly offered to collect them. Some of these wet afternoons can be profitably spent making toffee for the prisoners.

X
PHOTOGRAPHY AND XMAS CARDS.

As the Xmas season approaches, we desire to inform you that we are making a speciality of Greeting Cards prepared from your own photographs.

These Cards introduce a personal element, and thereby give an added pleasure to receiver and sender alike. They are prepared with a suitable greeting, and a border of artistic design, carefully chosen to harmonise with the subject. In a word, they strike a note of daintiness, which will be greatly appreciated by relatives and friends at home or at the front.

As work of this description entails a considerable amount of time and labour, we are obliged to stipulate that we cannot accept orders for Xmas after December 9th. We therefore urge you to place your orders with us as early as possible, in order to avoid delay and disappointment.

Specimens, at 3/6 per dozen, or 28/- per 100, may be seen at all our branches.

D. T. EVANS,
CHEMIST,
30, Harbour Street, Ramsgate, and 5, High Street, Broadstairs.
PHOTOGRAPHIC DEPARTMENT.
X

THE Xmas Pudding
RAISINS — Good New Fruit 6½, 1lb boxes stoned 9½, Best Selected Fruit 10½, 7lb Original boxes as imported 5⅝ per lb.

SULTANAS — Good Sound Fruit 10½, Best Selected 1/-, Finest Quality in 1lb and ½lb boxes 1/2½ & 7½ per box.

CURRANTS — Good Sound Fruit 6½, Best Selected 8½, Choicest Quality in 1lb & ½lb sealed boxes 1/- and 6½ per box.

BEST MIXED PEEL — Lemon, Orange & Citron ½lb Washed ½lb boxes 6½ per box.

BEST REFINED SUET — ½lb Packets 6½ each.

WORLD'S FRUIT is not cooked in water but to the wash tub, but is cleansed by a new and fruitful drying process enhanced by hand and the flavour not impaired by moisture.

need not cost you more if you buy the fruit at the

WORLDS STORES — Pioneers of Popular Prices
Local: 11, HIGH STREET, RAMSGATE.
Branches: 61, NORTHDOWN RD., MARGATE.

P O W CHRISTMAS PARCELS

The parcels to be delivered to the prisoners will this year contain the following, 1 tin of salmon, 1lb cheese, 1lb sugar, 1 tin of herrings & tomatoes, 1lb of jam, chocolate, 1/4lb of cocoa, 2 tins of milk, 1 tin of pineapple, 2 tins of potted meat, 2 soup packets, 1 home made cake, 2lb biscuits, 1 jar of "anti vermin" cream, 1 bandage, 1 tin of boric ointment soap, 1lb margarine, & tobacco.

The parcels are still short of five Christmas puddings. The cakes were given by Mrs Devas, Wood, Brooks, Smith, Gladstone, Raven, Dawson, Latham-Tomlin, Wish, & Misses Raven & Holt. Mr Day has offered to nail up the boxes. Anymore personal additions can be added, but they must be at Barfield House by next Tuesday.

1917

BROADSTAIRS ACTION, HOW TO INCREASE FOOD SUPPLIES

The Council started off the year discussing how to get more land under cultivation under a new edict from the Ministry of Agriculture, giving them more powers in acquiring land for the duration of the war. The Council now had the right to take over any vacant uncultivated land, not including gardens, for the growing of crops. The Council were to be given funds for the supply of seeds & manure. As it was only possible to guarantee a crop for one year before the war was over, only seasonable crops such as parsnips, potatoes, tomatoes, beans, carrots, peas etc were worth growing. Broadstairs decided, unlike Ramsgate & Margate, not to encourage the use of the land for poultry or rabbits. Councillor Bing felt they aught to encourage the keeping of the family pig, but the rest of the Council though it best left to the experts.

A committee was formed of Councillors Pemble, Byron, & Bowie, & a large supplier of seed potatoes was sought.

> **URBAN DISTRICT OF BROADSTAIRS AND ST. PETER'S.**
>
> **THE CULTIVATION OF LANDS ORDER, 1916.**
>
> **MAINTENANCE OF THE FOOD SUPPLY DURING THE WAR.**
>
> APPLICATIONS are invited from Residents in the Urban District who are willing to undertake the cultivation of land (in allotments or otherwise), which can be acquired under the above Order.
>
> Such applications, stating the amount of land required and the position desired, should reach me not later than Monday, the 8th January, 1917.
>
> Further particulars can be obtained from the undersigned.
>
> Owners and Occupiers of Lands who are willing to let the same to the Council for the cultivation of food-stuffs, are invited to send particulars of such lands to me by the time above-mentioned.
>
> L. A. SKINNER,
> Clerk to the Urban District Council.
> Broadstairs, 28th Dec., 1916.

The Council also purchased a supply of luminous paint to paint all of the pillar boxes in the town, as these were considered to be "*a danger on these foggy nights*".

Four more baths & a hot water cistern were also purchased & erected in the store at the rear of the Council Offices at the Broadway. It appears that these were much appreciated by the troops billeted in the town.

On the 3rd January 1917, the '*Albion Hut*', as the new Y M C A hut was dubbed, was officially opened by Colonel Grant. Mr Hayes, the War Secretary for the South East, said that he had opened many such huts for the use of the troops, but this was the first time he had seen one opened in a gasworks. He thanked the Gas Company for the use of the converted washroom, & the local volunteers that were behind the project.

As more & more men were being called up, more & more businesses began to close down.

TRADE NOTICE.

7, Clarendon-road,
Broadstairs.

Dear Sir or Madam,

Having been called up for Military Service, I regret to inform you that I am compelled to close my Business in all Departments for the duration of the War, with the exception of the Undertaking Department, which Messrs. W. Blackburn & Son. of Broadstairs and Ramsgate, have kindly consented to execute on my behalf.

I thank you for your kind support in the past, and I look forward with much pleasure to be favoured with your esteemed commands on my return.

I am, Dear Sir or Madam,
Yours faithfully,
ROBT. S. GOODBURN.

NOTICE.

I WISH to inform all my Customers that, owing to the war I have closed my Stables at Red Lion Yard, St. Peter's, for an indefinite period, and have removed everything to GRAPE VINE YARD, READING STREET. 'Phone 108.

All orders will receive prompt attention sent to this address.

(Signed) **WILLIAM HARLOW,**
Jobmaster.

BROADSTAIRS CHILDREN'S NEW YEARS TREAT

The auction rooms in Crow Hill have been converted into a fairyland for the occasion of the annual children's party. They have been tastily furnished with evergreen, paper festoons, red, white, & blue bunting, & Chinese lanterns. 500 children between the ages of five & thirteen attended & were well looked after by the ladies who were all dressed in costume.

After tea, Professor Portland entertained them with Punch & Judy, followed by a marionette show, impersonations, & ventriloquism.

Games & races with prizes of boxes of chocolates & oranges caused much merriment. Punctually at 8pm Father Christmas arrived & presented each child with a handsome toy.

The children from further away were transported home by Mr Dixon, the Master of Ceremonies was Mr Phillpott, assisted by Mr Taylor & Mr Piggott.

During the week, (January 10th), the 5th consignment of waste paper, weighing 3 tons 15 cwt, has been sent to the paper mills. This brings the total collected from the town to 13 tons 1 cwt, increasing the War Emergency Fund by £58. Thanks must go to Mr Piggott & Mr Perry for the free cartage, the Thanet Electric & Tramway Company for use of their premises for storage, & the Broadstairs & St Peters Scouts for the collecting of the paper.

THE GOVERNMENT WAR SAVINGS SCHEME

A band of nearly 200 ladies & gentlemen are hard at work organising a War Savings Association in the town. All establishments, Churches, public works departments, schools, etc, employing over 5 people, are intended to have their own branch.

The first branch off the mark was St Peters Parish Church, which opened its vestry last Wednesday evening between 6 & 7pm so that payments could be made. A total of £10. 5s was paid in.

By the end of February over £400 had been 'invested' in the War Loan, or as it was dubbed the 'Victory Fund'. The list of affiliated organisations steadily grew to 25.

Power House & Tramway Co	St Peters Elementary Schools
Dane Court	Council Schools Broadstairs
St Peters Church Vestry	Fairfield V A D Hospital
North Foreland Golf Club	St Peters Mothers Meeting

Holy Trinity Church
Broadstairs Banks
East Kent Laundry
Mildredsbourne School for Girls
The Vale, (Congregational Church)
Christ Church Osborne Road
Broadstairs Gas Works
York Street Methodists
Broadstairs Elementary Boys School
Shop Assistants Broadstairs
St Andrews Church
Broadstairs & St Peters Council
The Cinema
Brondesbury School
Girls Friendly Society
Queens Road Baptists
Broadstairs & St Peters Philanthropic Society

Your Money or Their Lives.

"Shall it ever be said that we were willing to give our sons, but we were not willing to give our money."
The Chancellor of the Exchequer.

Give YOUR answer through your Bankers, Brokers, Post Office, or War Savings Association.

BROADSTAIRS AND ST. PETER'S WAR SAVINGS COMMITTEE.

Executive Committee:
LIEUT.-COLONEL GRANT (Chairman).
Dr. BRIGHTMAN, Chairman of the Urban District Council.
Mr. L. A. SKINNER, Clerk to the Urban District Council.
Mr. J. A. FORDE, Manager Thanet Tramways.
Mr. L. V. MOORE (Hon. Treasurer), Capital & Counties Bank, Broadstairs.
Mr. G. A. TAYLOR (Hon. Secretary); Headmaster, St. Peter's Schools.
Mr. E. S. LEWIS (Hon. Assistant Secretary), Farnley, Gladstone Road.

Each of the above or any Clergyman or Minister will give full information as to the joining or the formation of a War Savings Association.

We want hundreds of millions of pounds and millions of hundreds of pence and shillings.

Every household can and must find something each week to lend to the Government.

RIGID ECONOMY IS THE ORDER OF THE DAY

Each affiliated organisation had its own committee, & the way it worked was that the subscriptions, which could be any amount, were pooled together & invested in War Certificates. Most organisations bought 15s 6d certificates. For each one the Government would give £1 in return when the war was over.

WHICH?

— OUR MEN ARE **GIVING** THEIR LIVES. —
YOU ARE ONLY ASKED TO **LEND** YOUR MONEY.

Friday the 16th of February
is the last day for application for War Loan.

BUT,
Your payments to War Loan Associations are to continue indefinitely.

Every payment made ensures
SOME LIFE SAVED. SOME MUTILATION AVOIDED.
THE NEARER ENDING OF THE WAR.

BROADSTAIRS AND ST. PETER'S WAR SAVINGS COMMITTEE.

Executive Committee:
LIEUT.-COLONEL GRANT (Chairman).
Dr. BRIGHTMAN, Chairman of the Urban District Council.
Mr. L. A. SKINNER, Clerk to the Urban District Council.
Mr. J. A. FORDE, Manager Thanet Tramways.
Mr. L. V. MOORE (Hon. Treasurer), Capital & Counties Bank, Broadstairs.
Mr. G. A. TAYLOR (Hon. Secretary); Headmaster, St. Peter's Schools.
Mr. E. S. LEWIS (Hon. Assistant Secretary), Farnley, Gladstone Road.

January 24th, *Owing to the fact that the minesweeper have been landing more frequently at Broadstairs, the coffers of the fund to supply them with fresh fruit & vegetables, has been reduced to 2 shillings. In the nick of time, Mrs Raven received a donation of £2 10s from Mrs H Gullick from Christ Church at the Broadway.*

With a view of helping the scheme for the enrolment of women into national work, the women of Broadstairs & St Peters who have had experience with horses, & those willing to receive training with same, are asked to get in touch with Council Chairman Dr Brightman, at his home Apsley House in the High Street, as soon as possible.
Six women enrolled, but more were requested.

A new bye law came into force this month, (February), in Broadstairs, where occupiers were enforced to clear any snow that falls on any footway or pavement adjoining their premises as soon as the snow ceased to fall. A penalty of £1 was payable.
It snowed one week later, but there were no reports of prosecutions.

TRENCH DIGGING (7th Feb)
At the Council meeting this week, a letter was read out by the clerk from the officer commanding the Broadstairs Company of the Kent Volunteer Corps, stating that under new regulations, the men were required that one drill a month should be devoted to trench digging, & asked the Council whether they could see their way clear to lend the Volunteers some picks & shovels, to enable the Company to fulfil its obligations. They would usually only be required on Sundays & they would fetch the implements themselves.
The Council granted the request, but there is no mention of where the trenches were to be dug.
The Council were also asked to relax its attitude on pig keeping by the Board of Agriculture. This they did, but put the matter in the hands of the Sanitary Committee, *"To keep an eye on things"*.
Another letter, this time from Mr Piggott & Co on the subject of cartage, was read out at the meeting. He said *"Carts I have, men & horses I haven't. Most of my men are away at the Front, & any of my horses that were any good have been requisitioned by the War Office"*. He asked the Council whether they could extend the times of his contracts, (carting sand, chalk, flints, & bricks), or find him more men & horses.

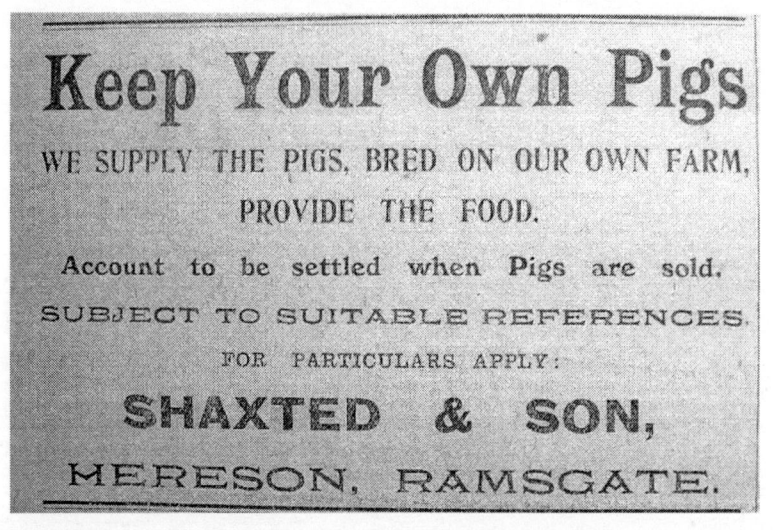

Keep Your Own Pigs

WE SUPPLY THE PIGS, BRED ON OUR OWN FARM,

PROVIDE THE FOOD.

Account to be settled when Pigs are sold.

SUBJECT TO SUITABLE REFERENCES

FOR PARTICULARS APPLY:

SHAXTED & SON,

MERESON, RAMSGATE.

February 19th, *a start was made on Monday evening, last, at the Bohemia rifle range, with a miniature rifle shooting competition for members of the Kent Volunteer Corps. The shoot was to be over 25 yards, & those who have won before are to be handicapped. A prize has been given by a local gentleman.*

On January 31st at the Area Military Tribunal at Canterbury, the driver of the Broadstairs Fire Brigade appealed against his exemption for war service being turned down. He was a single man aged 36, a four in hand horse & motor fireman, in the employ of a local jobmaster. Mr Whiteing his employer said he was ill himself, & the man was the only one left. He was doing an important job in the town, & if he left, his business would severely suffer without him.

The case was dismissed & the man was sent for immediate call up.

At the Military Tribunal in Broadstairs on February 11th, the case of the fire engine driver came up again, with a further appeal for more time. The Tribunal refused to discuss the matter, *"as it was now in the hands of the Military Authorities"*. Dr Brightman said,*"But we want the public to know that we are looking after their interests"*.

At the following Council meeting Mr W F Whiteing wrote asking to be relieved, at as early a date as possible, the contract for horsing the fire engine. This was as a consequence of the Military Tribunal decision the previous month, with respect to one of his employees (Mr William F Whiteing died a few days later, four days after his 79th birthday).

HOUSEWIVES MEET AT CINEMA

At the meeting this week, (Feb 14th) at the Cinema, an address *"Food & the Home in Wartime"*, was given by Mrs Cole. *"The war rations"*, she said, *"can be summed up in two words, NO WASTE, but in spite of the restrictions, people need not have fear for themselves"*. She was present this afternoon to show them that they could remain *"fat, fair, & forty"* & still obey Lord Devonport, (the Food Minister), at the same time. By giving up roast beef, egg puddings, & other savoury items, one might leave more of these things on the National Menu for the wounded boys in hospitals. She then went on with an interesting discourse on food values.

On February 28th, a party of children, who had received injuries & shock in the great East End explosion, were at the Metropolitan Convalescent Home in Lanthorne Road, where they were regaining their health & strength.

On the 28th February, the "Broadstairs & St Peters Mail" reported
SHELLED FOR 10 MINUTES
BROADSTAIRS & MARGATE UNDER FIRE
A MOTHER & TWO CHILDREN DIE, ANOTHER CHILD INJURED

For ten minutes on Sunday evening, (25th), Margate & Broadstairs were under fire from hostile destroyers, which appeared some distance off the coast at around 11.15. One woman was killed at Reading Street by a shell which struck her house, & her baby was so badly injured that it died within a few hours. Two other children of the same family aged 9 & 7 years respectively were seriously injured, one succumbing to her injuries at Margate Cottage Hospital. Two houses were wrecked & ten others destroyed.

Sir Edward Carson, First Lord of the Admiralty, said in a statement, one of our destroyers encountered a force of several enemy destroyers around 11pm, & a short engagement ensued. Our destroyer was not damaged though under heavy fire from guns & torpedoes. The enemy vessels were lost in the darkness. At about the same time, another force of enemy destroyers bombarded areas of Margate & Broadstairs. As soon as the firing was heard our forces in the vicinity were called to the scene, but the enemy had already departed.

OUR REPORT
The first intimation the residents in Reading Street had of anything untoward at just after 11pm, was when a shell whizzed through the air, to burst with a terrific explosion.

The first one found its billet in a semi-detached cottage in Reading Street. It penetrated the wall leaving a hole between two & three feet in diameter. Bursting in the bedroom, which the wife of the Government worker occupied with her young child, the shell wrecking the interior, killing the mother & seriously injuring the child who died shortly afterwards. Two other children, who were in another room, were also seriously injured.

The mother of the deceased woman lives on the other side of the road, with two other children of the family, & is naturally grief stricken.

Lord Northcliffe, who is staying in the area, sent his motorcar to take the injured to Margate Cottage Hospital.

Another shell burst 400 yards away felling a tree. Increasing the range of its guns, the enemy fired several other shells, which landed three or four miles away, on rural parts of Margate. One lady in Reading Street ran out to comfort an invalid friend, & in the course of the firing, a shell landed nearby, & splinters fell on her as she opened the door of her friend's residence.

Leading Stoker Edward Bing, brother of the dead woman, was at home on leave & rendered assistance at his sister's house after the shell had burst.

There has been an incessant flow of sightseers to Reading Street, some coming from quite some distance away.

The dead girl was Doris Morgan aged 9 years, & her baby sister was Phyllis Frances Morgan aged 20 months. Their mother was Daisy Agnes Morgan aged 40. Sydney Morgan, aged 7 is in Margate Cottage Hospital suffering from stomach injuries.

Dr Frank Brightman immediately started an appeal fund & Lord Northcliffe contributed £25 to start it off. William Johnson, a Reading Street resident, said, "As the general public will know by this time, one family suffered most severely. We were all in great danger, & it seems very hard that it should be the fate of one member of the community to have to suffer so much, whilst others have escaped, hence I am of the opinion that we should all do something practical to help. We should all show our gratitude for our providential escape".

THE INQUEST

At the inquest held in Margate five days later, Frank Horace Morgan said that he lived at Farm Cottage in Reading Street; he had been working away at Stonar, but was home that Sunday. He had a total of nine children, & on the Sunday night his house was hit by a shell at around 11.15pm. His wife had gone to bed about quarter of an hour before. He was downstairs & heard an explosion & came to the conclusion that it was a shell bursting. He looked through the window & saw the illuminations out at sea. As he heard no noise from upstairs he thought his wife & children were all asleep. He then went to the front door but was prevented from going outside. One of the shells had hit the brickwork making a thudding sound. The children were awake screaming. The oldest boy came downstairs screaming, & he sent him to his grandmothers. The wife with the baby in her arms started to come downstairs & he ran up to meet them. He carried one of the children downstairs & put him in a place of safety. His wife had got to the top of the stairs & he told her to hurry down, she replied, "I cant, I am hurt".

One of the bedroom walls, which had been struck by the shell, was completely wrecked.

THE EDITORIAL COMMENT

It was in keeping with the callousness of the enemy that they should shell such places as Broadstairs & Margate. No doubt the crews of the vessels concerned went back to their lair in Germany gleefully to announce to their compatriots that they had bombarded the fortified town of Broadstairs. No doubt Iron Crosses will be liberally bestowed for the accomplishments of this murderous errand. We cannot find words strong enough to express our contempt for these baby killers.

The house was renamed "Remembrance Cottage", & a feature was made of the hole where the shell went through.

There was later speculation that the shell was intended for Elmwood, the home of Lord Northcliffe, who was Minister of Propaganda at the time, but this has been discounted.

The funeral took place at St Andrews Church five days later. The hamlet church was crowded as the coffins were placed in the chancel. The joint choirs of St Andrews & St Peters were led in by Mr Battershall with the processional cross. The cortege then wound its way slowly to St Peters churchyard where the internments took place.

The *"Morgan Relief Fund"*, started by Dr Brightman was closed on March 14th, three weeks later. A total of £88.1.6d was contributed, amongst the contributors were, A Widows Mite 2/6d, A Grateful Schoolboy 1/-, & a Sympathetic Sister 1/-.

On March the 1st, the enemy were at it again.

UNWELCOME HERALD- HOSTILE AVIATORS VISIT

The following communiqué was issued by the Commander in Chief, Home Forces.

At 9.30am today, a hostile aeroplane dropped some bombs on Broadstairs. One woman was slightly injured

The *"Mail"* reported on March 7th

The weather was brilliantly fine at the time & there was little wind. The aeroplane flew at a great height & the first warning was the noise of the high powered engine coming from the sea.

Three bombs fell in the yard of the infant's school, shattering many panes of glass. None of the children were injured, but one teacher was slightly cut. The whole of a wall close by was peppered with holes.

A dog which was chained up in a yard close by was set free by a splinter of one of the bombs snapping a link in the chain.

Dr Brightman, the Chairman of the Council, had a lucky escape. He was walking on the seafront at the time. "The earth all around me seemed suddenly to rise, but I am not hurt as you see", he reported.

The school in question was the Council School, now St Mildreds & the dog was in Clarendon Road. The Council gave the children a week's holiday so the school could be repaired; presumably the dog also gained its freedom.

On March 7th, the "Mail" received a letter from Mr D Mason, the owner of the "Maisonette" in the High Street. He writes,

"*In connection with Christ Church in Osborne Road, it is proposed to hold a bazaar in the hall in Grosvenor Road. All the money received will go to St Dunstans Hostel for blind soldiers.*

The thought of young men being pitched into sudden darkness & not to realise the beauties of nature again & see ones friends again, is one of the most awful calamities that could befall these men. They have given all that is bright for their country.

Therefore I appeal to your readers to give any trinket, ornament, & articles of needlework to the bazaar. Gifts will be received on Monday evening between 6.30 & 7.30".

March *21st*   INVISIBLE ZEPPS

In the Kent coastal towns, over which the zeppelins flew last Friday night, there was little or no excitement amongst the populace.

With patches of low cloud in the sky at a low altitude, & the weather perfectly clear, the conditions were favourable to the raiders. In the three coastal towns the sound of engines was heard by watchful residents, but the noise soon died away.

Searchlights were brought into play, & it was weird to watch these probing fruitlessly the clouds looking for the raiders. As the noise of the engines died away, the lights were shut off one by one, leaving the watchers staring into the night sky. From a distance came a flash followed by muffled reports. Bombs were being dropped, but found their way into fields around the Dover area.

Members of the V A D, (Voluntary Aid Detachment), Men's Section, who have passed their first aid examinations, have now been equipped with serviceable haversacks, the contents of which consist of all that is needed to meet any kind of emergency. White brassards bearing the Geneva cross have also been served out.

DOING THEIR BIT

The boys of Alexander House School in the High Street have commenced a school garden for the cultivation of vegetables, at an allotment site at the bottom of Luton Avenue. Each boy is anxious to do his bit for the war effort. Senior boys are each responsible for one perch of land, 24 feet x 12 feet. There is keen competition between the boys, to see who can make the most productive plot.

MILITARY & THE LIGHTS

At the Cinque Ports Court on Monday, Bombardier Thomas Gordon of 5 Chandos Square was summoned with an offence against the lighting regulations. Sergeant Haddaway of the Broadstairs Police, said at around 7.30pm, he saw an un-obscured light from a lamp with no blinds drawn. This was clearly being seen from the sea. The defendant stated that the lamp was shaded with a cigarette card advertisement, & he had not been supplied with any blinds yet.

The magistrate told him, "It is customary to nail a blanket over the window in these circumstances. Fined 5/-"

At the Council meeting of April 4th, Dr Brightman made references to the many schools, & people leaving the town. He said he hoped that when they realise how unnecessary their fears were, they would soon return. About three hundred houses are now empty, as well as a considerable number of hotels & boarding houses. He hoped many old friends would return & visit the town, not only for its bracing sea air, but because they knew that the place was becoming into a bad way. He urged the inhabitants to keep the town as bright & cheerful as possible, & show confidence in themselves.

On Saturday 1st April brought a day of hail, sleet, & icy winds to the district. On the Sunday morning heavy clouds descended over the town, & for a period of one hour in the afternoon, snow fell in monster flakes.

KILLING A GERM

There was an interesting article in Mondays national "Daily Mail", which quotes

"Dr Brightman, the wise Chairman of Broadstairs Council, who has done more than any man since Charles Dickens, for the amenities & prosperity of that quaint town, has now conferred another boon on the inhabitants, by his discovery of the instantaneous treatment for the common disease of spreading wild & silly rumours, which he has dubbed the Rumour germ.

In that particular part of the coast which is subject to Hun activities, rumour has found a prolific breeding ground. People have heard, on good authority, a reported conviction all sorts of strange things, have seen strange twinkling lights in the sky & from the coast, & have detected perfectly innocent people in acts of treachery & espionage. These rumours, committed to Dr Brightman, confidentially, occupy a great deal of his time as he sets out to investigate them.

It became necessary to find a prophylactic treatment to prevent the spread of these invective rumours & the good doctor took the matter in hand with remarkable success. As is the case of other diseases, it appears the only way to combat rumour is to kill the germ.

The doctor discovered that the Rumour germ, which is of a vague, indefinable shape, & is conveyed in half spoken form by the breath of mouth, sometimes disclosed behind a half closed hand, is rendered completely innocuous by being reduced to writing.

In his office & library at home, "Apsley House", he has placed on a table a writing pad & pencil. When any of his good intentioned acquaintances come to him & say, "I think it is my duty sir, for your own information, I have heard on the best authority... ... ..." & so on, the good doctor interrupts the recital & says, " I am very much obliged to you for the information, but could you possibly write it down & sign your name". The informant would usually gaze at the blank sheet of paper, & the Rumour germ would be dead on the spot. There is not one of them that will put it in writing & sign his name, said the doctor.

His discovery has added to the cheerfulness of the town".

Seed Potatoes.

PLACE YOUR ORDER TO-DAY.

Our Stocks are running low. There will be a great shortage.

We appear unable to get further deliveries from the North.

SHAXTED & SON,

HERESON, RAMSGATE.

FINDING SUBSTITUES
FOOD ECONOMY AY BROADSTAIRS

On Saturday (April 18th), the first of six weekly demonstrations in war cookery is to be given at the Council Schools in Broadstairs. Admission will be by ticket only.

Discussions & demonstrations will be held on finding substitutes, such as that now rare luxury, the potato, & that other dwindling necessity, wheaten flour.

Every woman in Broadstairs will now have the opportunity of seeing what can be done, & will have the privilege of hearing an expert solve many of their pressing problems. One feature of the demonstration will be of the "hay box", which unlike gas does not need the stimulus of pennies-in-the-slot to make it work.

The "Mail" reported on the 25th of April,

The Grand Hotel is to be occupied by Canadian Officers the residents of Broadstairs will learn with great pleasure. The hotel has long been vacant as a result of the war. We understand that the use of the extensive building has been secured by the Canadian Authorities as an annexe to the Granville & Yarrow Hospitals, which are almost exclusively used by Canadian soldiers. We understand that the building is being converted & will in use within a month.

AMATEUR PHOTOGRAPHERS BEWARE

At the Cinque Ports Magistrates Courts, Miss Alice Carnley, a teacher residing at Broadstairs, was charged with taking a photograph contravening the Defence of the Realm Act on March 24th.

Sergeant Haddaway saw the defendant at around 7.50pm at the North Foreland, & asked her if she was the young lady who had taken a snapshot of a gun, mounted on a railway truck at Broadstairs Station on the 24th March. She admitted taking the photograph.

Inspector Ford produced in Court the offending photograph & negative. He said he did not imagine for one minute that the lady had taken the photograph for any improper motive, but at the same time she was not ignorant of the rules that the fact of photographing & sketching within one mile of the coast is strictly forbidden.

The bench said that they considered the offence a serious one & a fine of 10/- would be inflicted.

Through the energies of Mr H Ames an old disused retort house, adjoining the Y M C A Albion hut, has been converted into a "garden terrace" for the use of the troops for the summer months. Apart from the usual display of flowers, runner beans are being grown in the boxes.

PATRIOTIC BADGES

Another humble insignia of patriotism is now appearing in the windows of many local residents. This is the Food Controllers card, "IN HONOUR BOUND", a pledge limiting the household consumption of foodstuffs. This is similar to the "NOT AT HOME" displayed in the early days of 1915. Now the housewives of Broadstairs are battling the Hun in his endeavour to starve us out.

At the Council meeting of May 9th, a letter was read out from eight of the road scavengers employed by the Council, asking for an increase in wages. They pointed out the high cost of living, & stated that they had not received a regular war bonus like some other Council workers. The matter was referred to the General Purposes Committee.

Another circular was read out asking for the Council's support to encourage housewives to sift their cinders. The Clerk observed that most housewives in Broadstairs already did.

A request from the town's cinema to show the film "David Copperfield" on a Sunday was turned down, as the picture was not a sacred one. The Council does not want to show precedence on the subject.

The next big event in Broadstairs was St Dunstan's Week on the Whitsun bank holiday

FOR THE BLIND SOLDIER

Does the picture of the Blinded Soldier appeal to You ?

"If not, then shut your eyes for a few minutes when walking by the sea and say to yourself,—Suppose I was never to see again, never to see those faces that were dear to me. Then imagine what our men sacrificed when the world went from them in a rush of wind and flame."

HARRY LAUDER, in the *Sunday Herald.*

SPARE A GIFT OR COIN FOR ST. DUNSTAN'S WEEK.

SPARE A GIFT OR COIN FOR ST. DUNSTAN'S WEEK.

HOUSE & GROUNDS OF "MAISONNETTE,"
64, HIGH STREET, BROADSTAIRS,

OPEN WHIT-MONDAY & TUESDAY,
From 2.30 to 5.

FOREIGN BIRDS. VALUABLE CACTI COLLECTION.
CHERRY TREES IN BLOOM IN JAPANESE GARDEN.

There will be on view two deeply interesting mementoes—the Raft from the Lusitania, on which eleven bodies were washed ashore off the coast of Ireland, and the lifebelt which was saved from the German cruiser "Blucher."

ADMISSION 6d.

MANY TREASURES INSPECTED BY PATRONS OF BROADSTAIRS FETE

The Band of the Northumberland Fusiliers
will be in attendance MONDAY & TUESDAY
(By kind permission of the Officer commanding).

BAZAAR on WEDNESDAY and THURSDAY,
WHITSUN WEEK,
CHRIST CHURCH HALL, GROSVENOR ROAD
(One minute from Railway Station and Tram Terminus.)
Open 2.30. ADMISSION 6d.

All monies taken will be forwarded to St. Dunstan's Hostel for the Blind Soldiers. No deductions whatever for expenses incurred.

Brilliant sunshine, tempered by light breezes, made the ideal conditions for a garden fete on Whit Monday, & those who visited the "Maisonette" in the High Street were delighted by the variety of shady nooks, green lawns, & glorious foliage. Additional pleasure was provided by the band of the Northumberland Fusiliers with a selection of rousing tunes.

St Dunstan's Week commenced under very happy conditions & the owner, (Mr Dan Mason), is to be congratulated upon the assured result of his efforts.

The house is bound up with Royal historic associations with the town, & the original part dates from 1822, & was built by the Duchess of Kent for her daughter Victoria. In those days it was called the "Little Maisonette", but the largest part of the structure was added some considerable time later in a more modern style. The present owner is an ornithologist & botanist.

The lovely variation of blossom in the Japanese garden, the red Japanese fish lurking deep in the ponds, are offset by the old jackdaw who has a wire netting habitation at the bottom of an elm tree & a nest in the fork of the trunk. The gorgeous blue of the macaws in the aviary, & the second grove of songsters, & the quaintness of the multiform cacti are all sheltered behind the evergreen hedges of the central lawn.

It was curious amid this thoroughly English scene to see a boat of about 30 feet in length, elevated on trestles. It was the raft that floated ashore on the Irish coast after the "Lusitania" went down. Outside & inside the boards are painted a dismal grey, & one of the sides is pierced by a long shaped hole. A little plate on the stern told that it was made by a Glasgow firm, & was part of the "Lusitania". This is one of the most tragic relics of the terrible historic crises through which the world is passing. The raft's last voyage had 35 people on board, & when it reached the Irish shores eleven corpses were lashed to the benches. In the years to come, this simple vessel will be treasured for its association with that terrible catastrophe.

It is said that this sad memento may be offered to Broadstairs Council before very long. The present owner paid 110 guineas for the raft, & it has already raised over £1,000 for war charities.

A quick way of summing up the unique collection of art treasures in the public rooms of the "Maisonette", would be to call it the Broadstairs Museum, such is the array of artefacts. The dining room is tapestried from floor to ceiling & furnished with carved oak furniture of all descriptions. There is a life size Buddha carved in teak, & Japanese treasures abound. There are caskets carved with dragons, serpents, & peacocks, all beautifully carved & inlaid. There is also a wonderful Spanish cabinet with many holy pictures, a true marvel of workmanship. There are Dutch masters in profusion, mostly animal paintings, & old English portraits. There is also a pagoda in a bronze lacquer that took five years to make, cost several hundreds of pounds & is over 250 years old.

A large collection of porcelain is also housed in the rooms. Patriotic subjects such as Lord Nelson & Captain Hardy are captured in true naval style. There is also a man-of-war in a full suit of sails done in the quaint style of ceramic art. Another interesting item is a Chinese clock, where the hands stay stationary, & the dial rotates.

Outside, a stall of matchbox holders, made by the blind soldiers of St Dunstan's found ready buyers. Over 500 people passed through the turnstiles on Monday. Another good attendance was recorded on Tuesday.

The bazaar will be held in the grounds & not at Christ Church as advertised.

On the Wednesday, stalls were set up on either side of the drive approaching the house. The weather was once again glorious. A large marquee was set up in the grounds & used as a tea tent. Here visitors, whilst sipping their tea, enjoyed the wonderful views over Broadstairs & North Foreland, a view that the "Maisonette" is famous for.

The stalls were offering work done by the blind soldiers at St Dunstan's. All sorts of needlework & useful articles were on sale, being made by talented local ladies. A provisions & flower stall were so beautiful, no one could resist them. Even potatoes were on sale, selling out quickly at 1/- a pound.

On the china stall amongst other things were specimens of Japanese ware, a handsome brass clock, & a telescope. A cheeping came from a wickerwork basket which contained a drake called "Valentine", which was sold for ½ a guinea.

Under the hammer on Thursday, 5cwt of coal was sold for 11/-, & then was re-auctioned twice again in 1cwt lots. A shoulder of mutton fetched 6/- & was re-auctioned at 8/-.

At the end of the four days, a total of £203-10s-10d has been raised for St Dunstan's.

At the following Council meeting on June 6th, Dan Mason officially handed over the "Lusitania" life raft to the town; the council accepted the gift & thanked him for his generosity

The "Maisonette" stood in its own grounds covering approximately what is now Wardour Close. It is now called "Castle Gay" & is converted into flats. Dan Mason was the owner of the Cherry Blossom Boot Polish Company, & spent his money on charitable work including St Dunstan's, the West London Hospital, & the Salvation Army.

We have been asked, reported the "Mail", by the Council Chairman to state that if the official warning is received of a potential air raid between sunrise & 10pm, the siren will be sounded at Rumfields water works.

The signal will consist of three blasts each of five seconds, with an interval of five seconds between each blast. When the danger is past, the signal will be one long blast of ten seconds only. The siren will be tested every Saturday.

When the raid is imminent the inhabitants are warned of the extreme danger of being in the streets, & directed to confine themselves to their houses. People out of doors are also warned to seek shelter, & attention is called to the dangers of collecting of crowds, or watching in the open for aircraft.

UNINVITED CUSTOMERS, June 6th

Some amusement was caused on Tuesday morning in Albion Street, when a drove of sheep took possession of a stationers & newsagents shop. Luckily they put on their best behaviour & dodged the showcases with marked dexterity. Entering the premises by the shop door in Albion Street, they wandered into the library, & then out on the lawn of the premises facing the promenade. We cannot chronicle the remarks of the drover, but his flock had caused him a deal of anxiety prior to the raid on the fancy shop.

The minesweepers fund, which is used to purchase fresh vegetables for the minesweepers patrolling the channel, now has a new leader in the personage of Mr Dan Mason of the "Maisonette" in the High Street. All thanks must go to the originator of this excellent scheme, Mrs Hugh Raven. Broadstairs, we trust, will give the same generous support to Mr Mason as they did to his predecessor.

On checking the insurance taken out for the pier in 1915 against enemy action, the Council found that it was only covered for a sum of £500. The cover was raised to £4,500.

The Food Control Committee have secured a large supply of preserving bottles to store excess vegetables for the winter. These are of the Government pattern, & will cost 4s 6d per dozen, & can be used for many years. The instructions for use come with the bottles. Supplies will be from Mr George Taylor, "Lovejoy", St Peters.

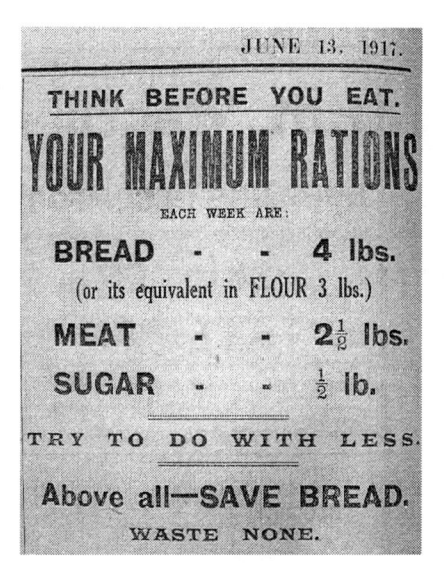

JUNE 13, 1917.

THINK BEFORE YOU EAT.

YOUR MAXIMUM RATIONS

EACH WEEK ARE:

BREAD - - 4 lbs.
(or its equivalent in FLOUR 3 lbs.)
MEAT - - 2½ lbs.
SUGAR - - ½ lb.

TRY TO DO WITH LESS.

Above all—SAVE BREAD.
WASTE NONE.

FELLS & SON, CASH GROCERS,
RAMSGATE AND BROADSTAIRS.

SUGAR DISTRIBUTION.

IN MARCH LAST WE INVITED ALL our regular customers to register with us their requirements of sugar under the voluntary rationing scheme. The great majority accepted our invitation, and all who did so have had their regular weekly supply without fail.

Under the Lord Rhondda Sugar Scheme of card rationing FELLS & SON invite you to nominate them as your Grocer for your weekly rations.

The dates to be observed are:
Distribution of Application Forms by post to householders, September 29th.
Applications to be received from public October 6th.
FELLS & SON to receive your Sugar Registration Card, November 5th.

We do the rest and you get the Sugar.

FELLS & SON,
94, HIGH STREET, AND 26, YORK STREET, RAMSGATE.
11, HIGH STREET, BROADSTAIRS.

DRINK FOR PATIENTS

At the Cinque Ports magistrate's court on Monday, Mrs Mercy Potts of 2 Staines Place Crow Hill was charged with supplying a Canadian soldier, undergoing hospital treatment, with a bottle of whiskey on the 11th June.

P C Day stated that whilst patrolling the town, he saw two wounded soldiers leave the defendants house in Staines Place at 3.40 in the afternoon, & one of them, named Mackay had something under his coat. Asking him what it was, he replied, "My laundry". Not being satisfied, he followed the two men to the Eastern Esplanade, & then managed to catch up with them near Victoria Gardens. On searching where the men had been standing, he found a bottle of whiskey. On questioning the men they admitted being soldiers being dressed in blue, (under medical treatment), at the Yarrow Hospital.

On questioning the defendant at her home in Staines Place, Mrs Potts said she only gave the soldiers some food. Finally she admitted getting them the bottle of whiskey for 3s 6d, because she needed the money to support her invalid husband.

She pleaded guilty & was sent to prison for two months.

The Yarrow Hospital had reported to the police the trouble they were having with their patients obtaining drink in the locality. The police were keeping an eye on several places within the town.

Arising out of the above charge, Mr A Holt, a grocer & wine merchant of 39 & 41 Albion Street, was charged with selling a bottle of whiskey without a label bearing his name & address affixed to it. He admitted the charge & was fined £5.

The police asked the magistrate for support to help stamp out what was becoming a very lucrative trade.

On July 11th, Pierremont Hall, one of the most prominent buildings in Broadstairs, was purchased by Mr Dan Mason of the "Maisonette".

On July 25th, the Misses Rolfe & Kelsey kindly offered their school "Mildredsbourne" (now Holyes Pine Emporium), to the local Womens Employment Committee as their headquarters. The offer was readily accepted.

The building was soon put to good use as the "Mail" reported on August the 15th

A WAR INDUSTRY

The Broadstairs & St Peters Women's Employment Committee are now in place in their headquarters at "Mildredsbourne" in the High Street. As part of the Government scheme, the hope has been expressed, that a small beginning to the industry, that is shirt making, would develop, & be the means of helping a good many persons to tide them over this difficult time, & assist in supplying the demand for underclothing for our fighting men.

The premises, during the last few days, has been the rendezvous for quite a number of seamstresses ready to receive instruction from Mrs Divall, (a Government Official), as to the most efficient way in making the shirts up. As soon as the work is passed as "satisfactory", they are allowed to take the work home. No restrictions as to the numbers of shirts put together is made, & it is hoped that those who put them together will produce as many as possible. The remuneration is 18 pennies per shirt; the cotton is to be provided.

The Central War Work Committee in London has looked to Broadstairs & St Peters to provide 1,000 shirts per week.

BROADSTAIRS

EMPLOYMENT FOR WOMEN AT HOME.

WANTED, NAMES OF WOMEN who are willing to do Government Needlework at their own homes.

Apply for particulars of remuneration, etc.,
Mrs. TAYLOR,
School House, St. Peter's.
Or Miss HOBBS,
30, Gladstone-road,
Broadstairs.

"LEST WE FORGET"

On Saturday, August 8th, a large number of people assembled on the old-world pier at Broadstairs, to watch the interesting ceremony of the unveiling of the ill fated "Lusitania" life raft, by Dr Brightman. Unveiling of the tablet, "LEST WE FORGET", the Chairman of the Council made a short speech on the meaning to the town of the gift from Mr Mason, who followed on with an address on how the raft came into his possession, & what his intended use for it was. Councillor Harry Bing, Chairman of the Pier & Harbour Committee, said he would assure Mr Mason & his fellow townsmen that he would see that great care was taken of it, & would see that it lost none of its lustre as the years rolled by.

65

The "Lusitania" life raft was mounted on the inside of Broadstairs pier, & was used successfully to raise money for First World War veterans. On its mast was a simple reminder, "Lest we forget". It was removed in 1939 & put into storage for the war period & replaced in 1945. It was removed again in 1949 to the town Council yard for maintenance & painting, when a lorry backed into it, rendering it beyond economical repair.)

Mrs Billie Perry a visitor from Fulham, was summoned on Monday to answer complaints from the Police of taking photographs in a prohibited area. On August 10th, she was seen by P C Horn taking a photograph of the Lusitania raft in Broadstairs harbour. It was admitted that no military importance was attached to the picture, but it was taken without Military permission. He requested the small Kodak camera she had used, & he confiscated the roll of film.

An inclusive fine of 10/- was inflicted.

MILITARY MEDAL PRESENTED AT BROADSTAIRS August 8th

A most pleasant function took place on Monday, when Gunner Charles Neave of a trench mortar battery of the R F A , was publicly presented with the Military Medal award, for bravery in the field.

Victoria Gardens was the venue, which was attended by the Northumberland Fusiliers, a large number of Canadian Officers from the Grand & Yarrow Hospitals, & patients from the local V A D hospitals "Roseneath" & "Fairfield".

The recipient was suffering from a compound fracture of the fibula & was accompanied by the Commandant of "Roseneath", Mrs F Brightman, & a number of her nursing staff.

Brigadier General R M Oven C M G, pinned the medal on the tunic of Gunner Neave, & said, "a man who earned that decoration in any other war, would probably have got a V C, but with 5,000,000 men serving there would be a great many men to be rewarded".

The action for which the award was made to Gunner Neave was at Wytschaete south of Ypres. The enemy made an unexpected bomb raid, & Gunner Neave immediately put his gun out of action & concealed himself in a bomb pit two yards away. The enemy threw grenades into the bomb store, but Neave was lucky to escape despite loosing his comrades. When the Boche had returned to their own lines, he left his hiding place, jumped to his gun, & meted out severe punishment. Between three & four hundred Germans took part in the raid.

Gunner Neave is a native of Norwich, & was a shoemaker before the war. He has been at "Roseneath" for eight weeks.

A squadron of about twenty enemy planes were reported over Felixstowe on the 15th August, & divided into two groups, some going in the direction of Clacton, the rest in the direction of Margate. Bombs were dropped on Southend, & some at Margate. The casualties from the raid were 32 killed & 43 injured. Things were now getting serious in the coastal towns.

THANETS ESCAPE DURING SUNDAYS AIR RAID

The majority of residents of Thanet were at tea, when they were disturbed by the shrieking of the sirens in each of the towns.

The sound of aircraft engines was heard almost at once at Broadstairs, & those who were in the streets & appeared at windows, saw flying at a height of 10,000 feet three black looking aircraft.

Firmly of the opinion that they were British, few people were concerned, & many resumed their disturbed meal. Within a few minutes, however, the gunners of the land batteries of anti aircraft guns realised at least one of the planes, which descended to a lower altitude than the others, was an enemy, & they opened fire. Seen through field glasses, this machine appeared to be of the Gotha type of battleplane.

Pursued by the puffs of smoke, which indicated the bursting of shrapnel, it travelled with the other machines still flying above, until it was near Ramsgate.

To those who inadvisably watched from the street, it appeared it was a miracle that the machine was not hit, but the majority were more keenly concerned as to the identity of the two smaller machines which hovered above, & which they were firmly of the opinion were British.

The view seems to have been substantiated when the Gotha suddenly fired a number of rounds from its machine guns, but the spectators were mystified when there was no answering fire. As the firing of the anti aircraft guns grew more intense, the spectators anticipated that bombs would be dropped, but either the raider failed to locate his objective, if those on board had one in view, or the shrapnel was bursting too close, & none materialised.

A short time later, bombs & aerial torpedoes were released whilst the raider was over the neighbourhood, a period that extended to five minutes. At the end of that time two other machines made their appearance over the water near Ramsgate, & the Gotha made off the direction of Margate. The others altered course & took to the same direction.

The two smaller machines, which constantly hovered above the larger one, also took off in the same direction, & the impression was that these were still British.

Meanwhile the residents of Margate had been disturbed by the firing & gained a view of the big machine as it reached the Cliftonville end of town. Further fire from anti aircraft guns was concentrated on it, & by this time it was flying over the "new town". Many more of our machines were in the air by now. The spectators were anticipating an aerial fight & forgot the dangers till they heard the sudden whistle through the air as a torpedo was released. A loud explosion followed as a total of four bombs were dropped. The aerial torpedo fell into the sea off Margate. The only damage done was to a house in Surry Road, where a house was totally destroyed.

The view of the residents of Ramsgate, Broadstairs & Margate was that they had another remarkably fortunate escape.

On August 27th the "Mail" reported

After the recent daylight raids on Ramsgate, Margate, & Westgate by Gotha bombers, the subject of bomb proof shelters for use of the general public was much discussed & considered by various Councils in Thanet.

Broadstairs & St Peters people had already taken to the use of some of the chalk caves in the vicinity.

In the vicinity of St Peters & Kingsgate, many excavations in solid chalk are to be found. Some are credited with being smugglers caves whilst others are disused chalk pits left over from lime working. Two such places were used as dugouts during Wednesday of last week, & many more with comparative ease & little expense, would make safe havens of refuge for the general public.

In the grounds of Hildersham House School a capital, & one could safely say, bombproof dugout is in existence, & was used by a few women & children on the 22nd inst. Our Broadstairs representative with Councillor Pemble as a guide paid a visit on Tuesday. The entrance is possible by a flight of a 20 step ladder in a crater, & a large excavation is at once noticed in the chalk beds. They are estimated to be at a depth of at least 16 feet, & run under the roadway of the village High Street, making them even more bombproof.

Another is situated in Victoria Road & is capable of housing 50 people. This has kindly been thrown open by the owner, Mr Charles Dennis, & was taken advantage of last week.

In the grounds of "Orlebar" in the High Street, (St Peters Old Boys), other large caves are to be found. There are several large caves in the Kingsgate area for the use of the Reading Street folk, whilst others are to be found at Bromstone.

The visitors on the sands this week, during the air raid, found the tunnel steps from the beach to the Victoria bandstand a place of security from the dangers of shrapnel, & great credit must go to the Council employees for marshalling the public. The excavations in the cliffs in the neighbourhood of Louisa Gap are other retreats, but unfortunately are not always accessible on account of the tides.

CANADIANS GOING – LOSS TO RAMSGATE & BROADSTAIRS, Aug 29th
Departure Hastened by Gotha Raids

By the end of the week, the whole of the Canadian Hospital patients at Ramsgate & Broadstairs will have been moved out of the district. It will cause regrets in both of these two towns. Following the recent air raids it was hinted that a removal was being considered, but the final raid over Ramsgate on the 22nd, has been decisive. The patients are being distributed amongst hospitals further inland. The staff will remain to assist in the removal of equipment & apparatus before moving on.

The Granville Hospital has 600 patients & a staff of 250. Chatham House School, which was opened as a hospital in 1916, has 250 patients & 100 staff. Townley Castle was also used as an annexe & has 50 patients. The Yarrow Hospital in Broadstairs has 150 beds & a staff of 100, & St Lawrence College accommodates 800 with a staff of 200, & is at present been renamed "Princess Patricia's Hospital.". The last building the Canadians took over was the Grand Hotel in Broadstairs which has 300 beds for convalescents & 150 staff.

Lieutenant General Clark said Ramsgate & Broadstairs were ideal places for the hospitals under normal circumstances. It was due to the men being wounded in France, however, to be put into a safer place when they came over to England.

On 22nd August there was another bombing raid over Ramsgate, this time at night. The Germans were more successful this time, & 9 people were killed & a considerable amount of damage was done. This pushed the idea of some form of underground public shelters further forward in resident's minds.

The "Mail" Editorial was on the side of the tunnellers.
RAIDS BY MOONLIGHT- Sept 5th

The men of the German Air Force, who specialise in baby killing & the ruthless slaughter of defenceless civilians to pander to their blood lust for murder of any description, appear to be making new ground & taking advantage of the harvest moon to further their wanton excesses. Their last two raids were conducted under these conditions. On Sunday night a single German plane paid a hurried visit to Dover, scattered bombs, & disappeared as quickly as it came. Fortunately even with the moon to guide him his aim was defective, & the toll of life & limb he was able to take was small, one man killed & six injured, which were all harmless civilians.

Monday nights moonlight raid was even less productive of result, seven bombs dropped on open ground, with barren results. What the raider did do in Thanet, on this his second visit, was to frighten a good many women & children, like the ugly bogey that he is.

All this gives added prominence to the question of bombproof shelters for civilians. From the correspondence that we have received, indicates there are two sides to the story. A suggestion to provide bombproof shelters has a large & probably immense majority of adherents. On the other side there are the people who apprehend a big element of danger to those who leave their houses to seek shelter elsewhere. Evacuation is also suggested by others, who however are in the minority.

Shelters to be effective will need to be numerous & easily available for people in a small area. This is however detail, with which others will have to follow, carefully & impartially, considering when the time is ripe for the taking of action.

TYPICAL GOTHA BOMBER OF 1917   max speed 83 mph

After Sunday 15th September, St Andrews Church in Reading Street will close, hopefully only for the winter months, the Vicar, Rev Mathews announced in this months Parish Magazine. He says, "I am afraid this has become a necessity, but the alarming overdraft on the bank leaves us with no alternative. We cannot afford the stipend for a third curate, (after St Peters & Holy Trinity), & the increased expenditure on lighting & heating".

On the subject of dugouts, the Vicar gives thanks to Mrs Raven at the "Coves" in the High Street, (St Peters), who has most kindly invited as many people from Church Street to take shelter at the "Coves" during air raids. "I am at present", the Rev Mathews writes, "asking for an estimate as to the cost of making the caves at the Vicarage bombproof. When this is done, shelter for those in Vicarage Hill & Calva Cottages would be provided for. Hopefully the people in & around Sowell Street will be able to use the dugouts at Selwyn House & St Peters Court.

Is it possible for the Council to obtain a grant from the Government towards the cost of providing these shelters"?

PROHIBITED PETROL

At the Cinque Ports magistrates court on September 5th, Henry Chalk & Frederick Arnold, the first a garage proprietor & the other a licensed hackney carriage driver, were summonsed for the illegal use of a certain motor spirit, against the Defence of the Realm Act 1914. This clearly stated that motor spirit was not to be used for ANY purpose of a motor car except & unless for ambulance hospital working, naval & military purposes, medical practioner, or munitions worker. Any other use would be deemed guilty of an offence & liable to conviction.

P C Parsons said, "At 11am Saturday August 8th, he saw two motor cars standing outside "Denemount" in Vale Road. Chalk & Arnold were the drivers. He asked them whether they had been 'ordered' for the wedding, which they said they had. They both made three journeys each to St Peters Church & back again, a distance of about six miles". He told them that they would both be reported.

Mr Chalk claimed that when he brought his present garage business just before the war, he also brought privately, a quantity of motor spirit, & this he kept quite separately from his business supply. He held a quantity of petrol on his private property which had been there since before the Act came in force. In his garage he was only allowed to store 72 gallons. On August 18th he had 60 gallons at the garage. He also had 5 gallons in his summer house in Broadstairs. At his home in Kingsgate he had another 20 tins of petrol in his tool store. He claimed that any difference between his allowed supply of 72 gallons & the 60 that he had for his business, was probably due to evaporation during the summer months.
He was convinced that he would be all right using his petrol from his private store. The magistrate said, "The order says, no motor spirit is to be used, no matter what its origins are".
Both were fined 5/- each.

Over the months of September & October, the residents of the town started digging with some earnest. Further raids had been made on Ramsgate & Margate in the previous two weeks.

BROADSTAIRS & ST PETERS GOES UNDERGROUND

A start was made this week by the residents of Beacon Road in providing themselves with a dugout. The offer of a piece of land came from Mr John Steed of Eagle House, Beacon Road. The two main entrance drives will be three feet, with a 4 feet blockhead, & three feet return. The main chamber will be four feet wide, from which niches will be cut out for each individual. The work is being carried out enthusiastically by volunteers, to the scale & plan drawn by an expert. During the last week an energetic band of workers has been using picks & shovels, & have turned the Victoria Road tunnels into a veritable fortress. There are now brickwork steps going down to the caves, & an additional stairway cut in the earth, & a handrail suitably fixed. These old disused chalk pits have been cleaned out & all the rubbish removed, & are estimated to be at a depth of 50 feet. Sand bags have been placed at the entrances & other improvements have been made for the refugees. The work is progressing under the supervision of Messrs Danton & Olive, & Messrs Piggott & Harrison have been carting sand. Bags or old sacks are urgently needed as well as old forms & chairs. It is estimated that between 200 & 300 people will use the accommodation. On a recent occasion over 200 people used it.

(Some of these tunnels collapsed in 2002 after construction work on three blocks of flats in the area).

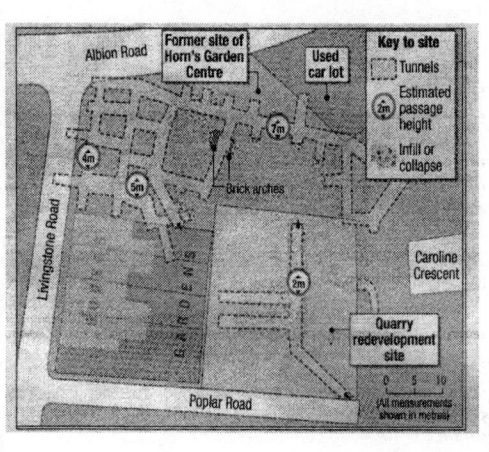

The Council approached the military seeking help, & with two squads of 15 men, were busy tunnelling under most parts of Broadstairs & St Peters. The surveyor was asked to look at the tunnels from the "Coves" & "Selwyn House" as both went under public roads. Otherwise there seems to have been little supervision or intervention of what was dug. There was still a small amount of opposition to digging tunnels using the argument that as so far no one had been killed in Broadstairs during an air raid, it was an awful lot of effort for no reward. After another two moonlight raids over Thanet, the digging became frenetic, & the Council was able to issue a list of the tunnels & their progress so far. Routine inspections were called for, weekly disinfections carried out under the auspices of the Sanitary Committee, & the Council called the owners of the donated lands together to draw up some semblance of rules.

On progress so far, (October 10th), the Chairman of the Council read the following report,
"Firstly the great difficulty at present is the scarcity of suitable labour, but thanks to volunteers, private enterprise, council workers, & the soldiers, we shall soon be able to say we have places for all those who want to use them.

The dugouts in St Peters Boys & Girls Schools are progressing well, & are to be used by the pupils & teaching staff during daylight raids. The large caves at the "Coves" in the High Street, (St Peters), owned by Mr Snowden, (Hildersham House), & Mrs Raven have been considerably improved & will now shelter 400 people. The caves in Victoria & Speke Roads form an excellent shelter for 300 persons. The underground passage at Selwyn House is a very popular shelter for around 100. At the corner of Edge End Road, Mr Piggott is constructing a dugout. The Council has now opened a large dugout shelter at Gladstone Road, which, when finished, will accommodate 500 persons. The old reservoir at Crampton Tower has been strengthened & will shelter 200. Another shelter is being dug in the Council Yard for the pupils of the Council School, (St Mildreds).

At Holy Trinity, the Rector shelters the pupils from the school underneath the vestry. The Council workers are now constructing another tunnel at the allotment end of Alexandra Road. The Council has also opened up the tunnel at Chandos Gardens, & another entrance is under construction at Waterloo Stairs. This will accommodate 400 people. 450 people have already been using the basement of the Grand Hotel when danger arises. There are private dugouts in Westcliff Road constructed by Dr Moon, Mrs Wickham, & Mr Bottley. These will have to be ticket only, as they have limited accommodation.

The Yarrow Home will shelter between 30 & 40 people. In the High Street a dugout for public use has been constructed at Dr Brightman's home "Apsley House". Another tunnel is being constructed at Crofts Place. There are also dugouts & tunnels at Kingston Farm, Upton, & Bromstone being constructed.

At "Eagle House" in Beacon Road is a newly constructed dugout, & others are at East Kent Laundry in Albion Road, Trinity Square in Reading Street & "Convent Cottages". "Brondesbury" School at Kingsgate, "Bruce Lodge", "Ivydene", "Tonglin", "Bishopsbourne", Sacketts Hill Farm, "Rimpton" & "Elmwood". The Council are about to start digging at land opposite the Infants School in Reading Street. In Stone Road there is a passageway at St Johns House of Rest. There are also tunnels being extended at Northwood & Westwood.

The Council would like to thank all those volunteers & workers, for all their hard work in constructing these tunnels. The owners of dugouts are being invited to a meeting with the Council to discuss a set of rules, such as overcrowding, & sanitary arrangements. The owners of tunnels are being asked to cover the chalk spoil tips with earth so they were not targets for bombers.

There are also demands being made that we use the siren to sound the all clear during the night. This we will discuss as a Council with the other two towns in the area. At present we see this as a good idea, & can see no reason why the sirens cannot be sounded anytime during the day & night time period".

Margate agreed to the idea a week later, & Ramsgate, after much discussion, fell into line another week after that.

A branch of the Girl Guides has been started, (Sept 12th), by Mrs Sandelman-Allen at "The Banks", St Peters. The aim of the movement is to develop good citizenship amongst girls, teaching those services useful to the public & handicrafts useful to themselves, inculcating patriotism, courage, self reliance, thrift, health values & a sense of duty & honour. Every age & class of girl is welcome, cheery, healthy enjoyment & happy comradeship is the fundamental principles. An influential committee has been formed of local ladies interested in this scheme, & the first enrolment will take place on the 20th. The committee meets three times a week at headquarters, "The Banks", St Peters.

DRIVEN BY GAS
Petrol replaced in delivery vans.

Many new methods are now replacing old ones, but one of the most interesting, caused by the scarcity of petrol, is that of the propulsion of motor vehicles by coal gas.

An enterprising firm, Messrs Kelsey, confectioners of Ramsgate & Broadstairs, have introduced this innovation into Thanet, by converting one of their delivery vans to a gas driven vehicle.

The motive power, provided from the local gasworks gasometer, is contained in a bag neatly concealed in a wooden box fixed to the roof of the van, which consequently draws little attention.

We are informed that the new system is easy of introduction, cheaper than petroleum spirit, & that very little power is lost.

MOONLIGHT RAIDERS Sept 26th

Official notification was given that between 7 & 8pm, anti aircraft practice would take place, in the course of searchlight practice. This was in progress about 7.20pm, when people on the seafront became aware of other ant-aircraft fire further westwards accompanied by shrapnel bursting high in the air. The beams of the searchlight also shot straight up into the air, but it was not until the sound of aircraft engines were heard that the sightseers realised that the display bore more significance than a mere practice. Spectacular though it was, in ones & twos, & then in larger groups, as the sounds of the engines became louder, they began to leave their place of vantage, & seek cover.

Meanwhile those in the streets of the town had also heard the sounds of engines, & for a time remained unconcerned & gazed skywards. Suddenly the searchlights concentrated, & then the screaming of the live shells through the air & the vivid explosions in the sky, caused the spectators to turn & glance at one another, with a mute, unspoken question written on their faces, sought shelter. Momentarily the sounds of aircraft engines became louder. The air-raid sirens sounded, & with that, people melted away like ice in the sun's rays. One bystander is confident that he saw one of the aircraft pass through the rays of two *searchlights. He described it as being like a butterfly. The primary excitement died away within a quarter of an hour.*

The dugouts were soon accommodated to their fullest capacity, & those who used them expressed with lively satisfaction at their provision whilst eagerly awaiting the all-clear to sound. They were destined to wait until 10.30 before the welcome invitation was given.

Meanwhile those who had remained in the open near such shelters acted as "look-outs", but depending upon the keenest of hearing instead of their eyes to pose to the world below that the sky was temporarily clear. The bolder ones emerged after a short period of time, only to return once more when the whirring of engines were heard approaching.

No bombs were dropped, & no enemy aircraft were hit in the locality.

HIDING IN A CELLAR

At the Town Hall magistrate's court in Margate were Private Stace Pritchard & Private Stephen Wickham who were charged with being deserters from the Buffs Regiment.

P C Haddaway stated that on the previous morning in consequence of information received, that there were two men, believed to be hiding in a house. He searched No 17 Speke Road St Peters, & found the two men hiding in the cellar. He took them to Broadstairs Police Station where they were charged.

The men were handed over to the military escort.

On October 7th, Dr Brightman & Captain Gladstone R N, started off another shilling fund for all the Broadstairs & St Peters soldiers, sailors & prisoners of war to receive a Christmas present. "Last year when the conditions were very much better than they are at present, the sum of nearly £100 was raised. This year it is computed to be only half of that amount will be necessary, in view of the fact that the gift to each man is merely to take the form of a pocket book & an almanac, two very useful articles for either a soldier or sailor".

As The Broadstairs & St Mail Wanted the Bombing

On October 10th, it was announced that the V A D Hospitals in Thanet would be temporarily shutting down, including those at "Roseneath" & "Fairfield" in Broadstairs. This was due to the prevailing conditions. *"It is surely unfair to men whose nerves have been so severely tried out on the Front to let them stay. This is not a local decision".*

By October 24th "Fairfield" was opened again, this time as a home for servicemen.

COFFEE INSTEAD OF TEA

We would refer our readers to recent advertisements of the International Stores, urging the public to use more coffee & drink less tea. Stocks of the latter commodity are comparatively short, but a great relief will be found, & a national service will be rendered, if the public will alter their "breakfast table".

> **Drink Coffee for Breakfast.**
>
> DURING the next few months there may possibly be a shortage of Tea. It is one of the little inconveniences we must suffer on account of the war, but the difficulty can be overcome by drinking Coffee instead of Tea.
>
> **Pure Coffee - 1/6**
> Delicious and Refreshing.
>
> **Pure Coffee - 1/8**
> An Ideal Breakfast Beverage.
>
> **SUGAR DISTRIBUTION**
>
> The official Sugar Cards should be distributed to householders before October 26th, and should be handed to your grocer before November 5th.
>
> If you will bring your card to us before November 5th we shall be pleased to arrange for your supply of sugar in accordance with the Government Scheme.
>
> **International Stores**
> THE BIGGEST GROCERS IN THE WORLD

UNIQUE PRESENTATION Oct 31st

A rather unique ceremony took place at the Victoria Road dugout on Monday evening, when the presentation of a silver watch was made to Mr Charles Dennis, the owner of the caves.

On Monday evening at around 10.45, the people in the area assembled at the dugout, when along came the Vicar, Rev C H S Mathews, (with his special constables armlet on), & his "prisoner", & by the expression on Mr Dennis's face, he appeared to be at a loss as to why he should be made to put in an appearance at that time of night.

The vicar, voiced his thanks from all those present to Mr Dennis on enabling the residents to use his caves as a place of safe refuge, & presented him with a silver watch for which they had all subscribed.

Mr Dennis replied that he had almost failed to recognise the caves for their destined purpose & thanked Mr G Danton & Mr Olive & others for all the hard work, & labour they had put in, improving the shelter.

The caves provide shelter for around 300 people.

Since the formation of the Girl Guides in Broadstairs & St Peters a few weeks ago, they now have 70 members enrolled, enabling them to form two companies. Number 1 Company parades on Thursday under Captain Mrs Allen, with Lieutenant Miss Gorston, & Number 2 Company meets on Saturday under Captain Mrs Fry, with Mrs Cornish as Lieutenant. Both Companies meet up on Sunday between 6 & 7pm.

The Guides meet at "The Banks" Bairds Hill, & a drill room has been put at their disposal at Selwyn House thanks to Mr Price. A fancy sale of work will take place on Saturday to raise funds for expenses & uniforms.

Over a quarter of a ton of horse chestnuts have been collected by the Guides for the Ministry of Munitions. The girls are also assisting the Scouts on the waste paper collections. Other useful work being done is the distribution of Government literature.

A BRAVE NURSE
Broadstairs Lady Decorated by the King

Sister Margaret Bowie, daughter of the late Mr Thomas Bowie of Elmwood Farm, had the honour of being received by the King at Buckingham Palace last week. There she was presented with the Royal Red Cross (Second Class) Medal. During the presentation, his Majesty asked many questions as to her experiences, particularly the part she played in the retreat of Mons in 1914.

The decoration was bestowed for her long service & devotion to duty. Made of silver, it is in the shape of a Maltese cross, with red enamel panels, & the Kings head in the centre. At the back is inscribed, "Faith, Hope, & Charity". It is hung with a bow of dark red ribbon with blue stripes.

Our readers will remember our account we gave of this brave nurses exploits in the autumn of 1914.

On November 21st, a statement was made in the "Mail" with reference to the closure of the V A D Hospitals in Thanet.

Little comment was made recently on the closure of the V A D Hospitals in Thanet, but a fine tribute was paid recently by Lord Chilson. Detailing that the hospitals were all closed by the War Office, "I should like to say on the part of the staff, that no member of the staff ever requested them to be closed down. They were all prepared to work there amid the almost perpetual air raids. I have never had a more painful day than when I went down there so say, "Thank you", to all those who have worked there over the last three years"

Since the opening of "Roseneath" & "Fairfield" Hospital in Broadstairs, they have treated a total of over 1,600 soldiers, who have been healed of their wounds, & nursed back to health. .

On November 21st, the Hon Treasurer of the St Peters Soldiers & Sailors Comfort Club, Margaret Raven of "The Coves", writes, "I hear that the soldier's relatives are disappointed that the men are receiving fewer parcels than formerly. I want to explain that as the subscriptions have gone down, & the price of goods, where obtainable, have considerably increased, we are only able to send 12 parcels each week, instead of the more usual 24. We have 100 soldiers on our list, & 59 sailors, so they cannot each get more than 4 parcels a year, unless funds significantly improve.

We have just received 20 pairs of socks from a Scotch knitting club, which will be included in the next round of parcels".

VICTORY PEALS November 28th

A correspondent writes, "Owing to the fact that the majority of the bell ringers of St Peters Church are either serving with the colours, or doing work of national importance, is it not possible to train a number of lady bell ringers to fill the vacancies? We should then be able to have a "Victory peal" when the time comes. I am sure our lady friends would be willing to fall into line".

THE SHIRT INDUSTRY December 19th

Excellent progress is being made by the shirt making industry of Broadstairs organised by Mrs Grant last July. Those engaged are very keen, & already over 2,300 garments have been completed.

UNITED ACTION
Thanet Efforts for Relief of Traders & Rates

The Broadstairs Council met a delegation of trades & townspeople on November 7th to discuss the relief of Rates & the general state of the things within the town.

Dr Brightman, the Council Chairman, reported that for the last two years he viewed with great unease, the terrible strain put on the town's finances which was the inevitable result of a long drawn out war. By exercising the greatest economy they had managed to keep their heads above water, just. So far he thought it expedient to carry on, making no references in the public press, but they now thought the time was right, & asked the town to support the Council on certain matters. For the last two & a half years, they had taken part in the East Coast Conference, which represents town Councils & businessmen in discussions with the Government.

As a group they had approached the Government to get relief for the rates, so far unsuccessfully. The only relief that they had managed to obtain was from the Canadian Relief Fund, of which Broadstairs had £3,659. Broadstairs was one of the very few towns that had lowered its rates. That has been done by cutting expenses to a minimum, which is what the Government required us to do. We now question whether that was the right decision. No money has been spent on roads etc, & we are now faced with a long winter after three hard summers, & we feel our case is a strong one, & we are appealing to the Government for assistance. The other two Thanet towns are in similar circumstances, but the Government will only talk to us through the East Coast Committee. For this reason we need to talk to the other two towns & create a united front. Margate & Broadstairs were already talking together on the subject, & no doubt Ramsgate will fall into line. With this aim we would like eight representatives from the town's traders, preferably traders of long standing, to meet representatives of the other two towns.

This hopefully will give us more say, & hopefully increase our chances of success on the matter of rate relief. As an example he then went on to quote figures from the Entertainment Committee

	Profit	Ticket sales at entertainment functions
1913	£3,086	208,002
1914	£3,322	210,230
1915	£1,567	
1916	£940	
1917	£439	33,292

TEN LITTLE AEROPLANES

Ten little Gotha planes, flying in a line
One did a nose dive, & then there were nine,
Nine little Gotha planes, stopping out late,
One ran out of petrol, & then there were eight.
Eight little Gotha planes, flying up in heaven,
One did a corkscrew, & then there were seven,
Seven little Gotha planes, in an awful fix,
One got in barrage fire, & then there were six,
Six little Gotha planes only left alive.
A monitor accounts for one of them, & then there were five,
Five little Gotha planes, leaving Britain's shore
An "Archie" gun sighted one, & then there were four.
Four little Gotha planes, oh how fast they flee,
One the channel tried to swim, & now there are three,
Three little Gotha planes, back to home they flew,
Commander "B" brought down one, & then there were two,
Two little Gotha planes, flying to the Hun,
One came down in Belgium, & then there was one,
One little Goltha plane, flying all alone,
He collapsed on landing, & then there was none.
                    Alfred Edgar Videan (aged 14)

A meeting was called by Dr Brightman on Monday afternoon, (December 19th), at the Council offices, & was well represented by the women of the town, where he explained to them the terms of enlistment of the services for war work to be done in Thanet.

The doctor said that the Military Authorities had decided to engage a certain number of women workers to sort salvage from the battlefields. The number from Broadstairs was to be about 50. The labour would be heavy, he warned, & shelter would be provided, one for working in, & the other as a mess room. Their meals would be prepared for them, & they would all work in gangs. The working hours were eight hours a day from 8am till 4pm in winter, & 10 hours a day in the summer. The remuneration was 6d or 8d per hour, & dinner hours would be paid for to cover the railway fare. Mr J Forde has kindly promised to run a tram to Ramsgate & a special train will leave from the Sands Station at 7.20am.

It is essential that they should be well shod, posses strong gloves, & it was recommended that trousers should be worn, (laughter).
He then went on to observe that in these war days, they were subject to many changes, & he was sure that the ladies would soon get used to their new attire.
We understand that many of the ladies present registered their names.

This was reference to work being done at Richborough Port, (now Pfizers), where almost everything military that went into, & out of France was transported. Women were employed to sort the salvage materials. 388,545 tons of salvageable material was returned from France between 1916 & 1919.

SOME OF THE LOCAL GIRLS UNLOADING SALVAGE AT RICHBOROUGH

RUNAWAYS December 24th

The Station gates at the Goods Yard, (Health Centre Car Park), *were considerably damaged on Thursday afternoon, when a pair of horses took fright & bolted with an army trolley, to which they were attached, was being loaded with coal. Opposite the passenger entrance, (up line), one of the horses fell. The jerk uncoupled the trolley & shot coal into the road. The two horses were eventually stopped at the corner of Edge End Road.*

As 1917 was drawing to a close, food was getting scarce, with fresh vegetables becoming almost unobtainable. Rice had taken over from the humble potatoes as part of the staple diet; sugar & tea were coming under official rationing schemes, & meat was rationed by the butcher, *"there was never enough of anything to go round,"* was a common complaint. The town's residents were now burrowing under the town like rabbits, as the coastal raids were becoming more frequent. Fortunately little damage was caused from by the raids, & apart from the Morgans in Reading Street, whose descendents still live in the area, no serious casualties were reported. Many people were still leaving the town, & with the withdrawal of some schools, & the local V A D Hospitals, the Canadians at the Yarrow, those left behind were constantly looking over their shoulders to see who was going next. The Council was often getting letters from places as far away as Devon & Scotland, asking them to purchase houses from people who had moved away. They were all declined.

The tram system was gradually falling apart due to a lack of maintenance, & the service was reduced drastically as trams were being taken out of service. Electricity was up in price by 10%, & gas was going up by 6d per 1,000 therms on the 1st January.

The cinema finally got its way & was able to show films on a Sunday, *only for the troops stationed in the town, & provided it didn't clash with afternoon or evening church services.* Twelve canteens for the troops were set up around the town, & another Y M C A hut was being installed at the Council Yard, (Crampton Tower). Keeping the Home Defence soldiers, who were billeted in the town, amused & occupied was a continual problem, as the cases of petty thieving, damage & trespass were being brought before the courts testified. Most of the churches now had some form of reading room for the troops, some even obtaining billiard tables. The last of the available men were gradually rounded up as the Military Tribunals at Canterbury overruled the local exemptions.

The Little League, the Minesweeper Fund, & Soldiers & Sailors Comfort Fund, were all struggling from a lack of money & supplies of material, but all kept going.

A few weddings took place at St Peters, between Canadian soldiers who had been at the Yarrow & local girls.

War work for women was gradually becoming a necessity, both as an income for the women, & a valuable source of labour for the Government. The "Shirts for Soldiers" industry in Broadstairs was a good example, as was the materials salvage at Richborough Port, where some 500 women from the three Thanet towns were employed.

Women still dreaded the knock on the door to find a Telegraph boy standing there with a telegram starting, *"We are sorry to inform you... ... ..."*

Things couldn't get any worse in 1918, or could they?

1918

The new year of 1918 "came in" very quietly in Broadstairs. The usual heralding of church bells & steamship whistles & buzzers were entirely absent. As the old year passed, the streets presented a deserted appearance.

In view of the state of the moon, the watch night services at the churches & chapels were all foregone. Generally there was an air of solemnity as the New Year began, most people wondering what it would bring forth.

By 2nd January the old boys of St Peters Elementary Schools had 327 men serving with the forces. One had risen to the rank of Major, seven had gained commissions, & three Distinguished Conduct Medals, two Military Crosses, & two Military Medals had been awarded.

Food was the predominant issue at the start of the year. Rationing was already in place, the allowances being margarine or butter 4oz per head, tea 1½ oz per head, sugar ½ lb per head all per week.
Lord Rhondda, (the Food Minister); had brought in rules for a distribution system of food at the end of the last year, & put the controls on the local food committee's for enforcement, backed by the courts. A fine of £100 or 6 months imprisonment was to be enforced for misuse of the new ration cards.

The main feature of Lord Rhondda's scheme was to even out the distribution of food & the elimination of queuing by

A   Every customer should be registered with one shop for the purchase of foodstuffs, & not allowed to buy elsewhere.
B   The shopkeeper shall be required to divide weekly supplies in fair proportions amongst the customers registered to him.
C   No shopkeeper should be allowed to register more customers than he can conveniently serve.
D   The supplies of any one article of foodstuff should be distributed amongst retailers in proportion to their registered customers, & the limit should be fixed as to the amount of any one item of foodstuff a registered customer is able to obtain.
E   A system of providing retailers with cards or slips, on which customers can register, will be shortly introduced. This work will all be done by the retailer, & not by the Post Office.

SCARCITY OF MEAT 2nd January

At Canterbury Cattle Market meat was so scarce this week that the allotment for Broadstairs was two bullocks, Ramsgate five bullocks, Margate five bullocks; pigs were also allocated. It was estimated that there were 120 butchers present & only 50 beasts to meet their demands.

By the 13th February, this had been reduced to one bullock & ten sheep for the whole of Broadstairs & St Peters, the lowest on record.

The new Y M C A hut at the Council Yard, (Crampton Tower), will be opened this week. It has been dubbed the "Station Hut", & is 99 feet in length, & 30 feet wide & will accommodate 500 men. At one end of the hut is a stage, complete with scenery & footlights, at the other end is a canteen, & a billiard table has also been installed. The building is lit by electricity throughout, & is efficiently heated. The main entrance is from Grosvenor Road, but access can also be obtained through the Council Yard.

January 9th. Mrs Edith Marian Brightman, the wife of the Council Chairman, has received by appointment, the honour, Member of the British Empire, (M B E), for her work as Commandant of Fairfield Auxiliary Hospital since the premises were taken over as a V A D institution.

At present there are no crèches in Broadstairs for women doing war work. About 50 women, several of them being single, leave the station daily for work elswhere, & so far the married women have made other arrangements for their children. If a crèche is required, Dr Brightman is confident that one could soon be established if requested.

The manager of the Cinema wrote to the Council this week, thanking them for allowing the troops to watch performances on a Sunday. He asked whether officers would be allowed to bring their friends, as the men liked to see their lady friends, & married men their wives on a Sunday.

Councillor the Rev Ridgeway asked how many friends would be allowed per man, but it was decided to leave that to the Commanding Officer on duty. Councillor Nash thought that it was a better idea for soldiers to bring their lady friends to the cinema rather than loiter around on the seafront.

The application was granted.

A LARGE MUSTER AT ST PETERS

Members of the 4th Battalion of the Kent Volunteer Reserve attended a divine service at St Peters Church on Sunday. The church was full to capacity, & there was not a vacant seat in the sacred place.

The Ramsgate Volunteers paraded at their headquarters at 9.30, & marched to Broadstairs, whilst the Margate Company did the same.

The Volunteers all assembled at Broadstairs Station Yard, the Battalion Brass & Bugle Band being present, played stirring tunes en route to the church.

The men made an imposing spectacle as they marched through the town, & it says much for their training that they have attained such efficiency & bearing.

ST PETERS CADET CORPS

A Cadet Corps has been formed by the lads at St Peters, the age limits being 13 to 18 years. A number of lads have received excellent army training under the instructor Ex Sergeant T W Davis. The Corps will be affiliated to the Kings Royal Rifles when the strength improves. Lads wishing to join should get in touch with Mr Davis at 33 Magdala Road St Peters.

The parades are held at the infant's school, Ranelagh Grove. The following orders give some idea of the training the lads will receive

Squad drill, topographical definitions, semaphore, marching by night, (if dry), & map reading. Uniforms will eventually be provided. So far 30 lads have signed up.

On January 9th, a quantity of sugar, tinned meat, & corn flour has been received by the Council from the Queensland Government, which will soon be distributed to the poor of the town.

Interestingly the bags of sugar bore labels "To the Mayor of Broadstairs".

DUG OUT COMPLAINTS

We have received a letter from a Broadstairs correspondent querying as to why there are no steps to provide a dugout in the King Edward Avenue area of the town. A petition was forwarded to the Council some time ago. & they promised that a dugout would be provided, but it would appear that the petition has been ignored. "It cannot be for the matter of land as there are several vacant plots in the area, & it cannot be for the lack of labour as there are countless soldiers billeted in the area who seem to have plenty of spare time on their hands. There is little doubt that the men folk of the neighbourhood would only be to glad to give a little spare time under experienced supervision in constructing a safe shelter. There is nowhere in this area other than the High Street, which would take women & children some considerable time to reach. Surely residents are entitled to a little consideration & protection".

Another letter signed a "townsman", asks for a shelter for the residents in the Rectory Road area. He complains that the upper part of the town at St Peters is well provided for, but the residents of the seafront have to go without.

CLOTHES & HAMMOCKS Feb 6th

Through the Vicar of St Peters & his wife, Mrs Matthews, a sum of money has been collected from friends in safe areas away from air raids, to purchase warm clothing for the children when taken from the safety of their homes during visits of hostile aircraft.

A working party has been making warm clothing, warm cloaks for the girls, & purchasing jerseys & warm sweaters for the boys. The articles have been given on the understanding that they are only to be used on air raid nights, & are to be kept in good condition.

It is interesting to learn that the articles have all been marked "D O", for dug out, & are only to be worn on that occasion.

We have been asked by the Vicar to state that he hopes to provide a number of hammocks in the near future, for the use of the children, & have asked for people to undertake "netting" the same.

The shop assistants of Broadstairs have in the past 12 months purchased £480 15s 6d in war certificates representing a total sum of £372. The membership registration is nearly 100 people.

FINDERS NOT KEEPERS

Two men, of the labouring classes, William Flanders of Church Square, & Thomas Laslett of Church Cottage Broadstairs, were charged with picking up a quantity of margarine on the foreshore at Broadstairs. One had 14 lbs, & the other 11 lbs which had been washed up on the sands. Asked on its condition, Coastguard William Richaby said, "I wouldn't eat it, it was all covered in sand & bits. I gather some of it had been "run down", to get the filth out of it, so it could be used in puddings or a bit of pie crust".

Both men were told by the magistrate, that in this case finders were not keepers, & bound both men over for 6 months with a £5 fine.

THREE SIRENS Feb 13th

A new electrical siren has been mounted on the Council Offices at the Broadway, which will be operated by the Caretaker Mr Bushell. As the lever is right next to the telephone, no time should be lost sounding the alarm.

The new siren is double ended & its trumpets point east & west, & can be heard as far away as Kingsgate, three miles away. The installation was carried out by Mr Vernon Hill, & the total cost including purchase was £100.

The steam whistle will still be used at the tram works in the event of an impending raid, & the siren at Rumfields will still be used.

On Saturday the "queue evil" was successfully disbanded by the Broadstairs Food Committee, under the powers conferred on it by Lord Rhondda. A portion of margarine on sale at a company shop, (chain store), was commandeered & redistributed to other retailers. The queue disappeared, as quickly as it formed.

The dugout at Crawford Road & the corner of St Peters Park Road was completed on Sunday, (17th Feb), & provided shelter that same evening & since. The shelter is an ideal one being well lighted & with seating accommodation for 100 persons.

The Council are still requiring volunteers to assist with finishing the dugout behind the Council Yard for the Council School children.

RATION CARDS Feb 20th

From information received from the Food Control Committee, we are able to state that the great bulk of food & meat cards have been filled up & delivered yesterday.

It is estimated that over 2000 application forms have been issued, 170 insufficiently filled in, necessitating their return to the applicants, delaying the issue of ration cards.

Several forms were returned with no name & address on them, whilst others have failed to fill in their favoured retailer's name. All cards should be handed over to the shopkeeper on the day they are received, so that he can ensure that he can include them in his returns of supplies required.

Any person not having a card properly filled in will prejudice their prospect of being served after February 25th.

Dr Brightman's Christmas Present Fund provided 557 presents for Broadstairs & St Peters servicemen serving abroad.

TO OUR CUSTOMERS

The system of Registration for various articles of food is being extended, and customers have to nominate the Retailer from whom they desire to draw their supplies.

We tender to our regular customers the assurance of the best possible service of their interests if they nominate our local branch.

Our assistants will be pleased to give customers any information they require as soon as instructions have been issued from the Local Food Authority.

International Stores
TEA :: COFFEE :: GROCERIES :: PROVISIONS.

On March 20th, the newly formed St Peters Cadet Corps was disbanded, owing to the difficulties of obtaining officers, & on account of financial problems. It is hoped to resurrect the Corps in the near future.

THE CURFEW April 3rd

A new Board of Trade Order, which aims at reducing the consumption of gas & electricity, became operative on Tuesday, (2nd), & was locally observed throughout Thanet.

Lights hve to be put out in all places of entertainment by 10.30pm. No hot meals may be served in any public place, hotel, boarding house, or club between 9.30pm & 5am. All dining rooms must be closed at 10pm.

No lighting of any description shall be used at anytime in any shop front except for illuminating a small sign indicating the shop is open. Light inside a shop for serving customers will only be allowed with Police approval.

Private customers of gas & electricity must watch their meters. They will only be allowed to consume 5/6ths of the amount they consumed in the corresponding quarter of 1916 or 1917, whichever was the greater.

BROADSTAIRS RAID SHELTERS.

The following official list of raid shelters in Broadstairs will be of general interest. The figures alongside each indicates the approximate number of persons the places will hold.

St. Peter's Girls' Schools, Ranelagh-grove, 400 (children).
" The Coves," High-street, St. Peter's, 250.
Caves at end of Victoria-road, St. Peter's, 150.
Gladstone-road, nr. Seafield-road, Broadstairs, 300.
Waterloo Steps and the Parade, Broadstairs, 600.
Aspley House gardens, High-street, Broadstairs, 120.
Reading Street, opposite Infants' School, 150.
Percy-avenue, Kingsgate, 50.
Albion-road, St. Peter's (Mr. Steed's Lime Works), 150.
Rumfields Gap, 50.
Underground passage at Selwyn Ho, St. Peter's-road, 50.
Crawford-road, St. Peter's, 150.
Alexandra-road, Broadstairs (under allotments), 100.

Dug-outs in Progress of Construction.

King Edward-avenue, Broadstairs, 100.
Town Yard, Grosvenor-road, Broadstairs, 100.
Rectory-road, Broadstairs, 150.

Dug-outs Proposed to be Made.

Victoria-avenue, Northdown, 50.
Mr. Nash's Field at end of Prospect-place, 100.
Total accommodation, 3,020.

The public are admitted to the following private shelters by card invitation :—
Upton Lodge, Upton (Mrs. Noott's).
Edge End-road (Mr. Piggott's).
Seapoint-road (Mrs. Wickham's).
Caves at Bromstone.
Bruce Lodge, Kingsgate.
Westwood (opposite Fern Cottage).
Dr. Moon's, West Cliff-road.
Cellars under East Kent Laundry.

The Completed Dugouts March 1918

THE DRILL HALL

The new Y M C A "Station Hut" was suddenly closed on 3rd April with no explanation, & re-opened on 17th April, & was to be known as the "Drill Hall" Broadstairs. It is now to be used by the various Volunteer regiments in the locality. The first drill was on the 24th & was a combined drill of the 3rd Volunteer Battalion, East Kent Regiment, (the Buffs), A S C Motor Transport, R A M C, & the Volunteer Corps all took part.

About 20 acres of land in Broadstairs is now being cultivated as allotments. A large number of the plots are worked by women, who are most enthusiastic.

The Council were apparently still struggling with the siting of the town's air raid sirens. A new siren, to replace the one on the Council Offices at the Broadway with one on Crampton's water tower, was relocated.

April 10th. The proposed new electric siren destined for Crampton Tower has found a new home over the premises of Timothy Whites & Co in the lower High Street. This has found favour with the inhabitants at the lower end of the town. The siren will still be controlled from the Council Offices at the Broadway.

June 12th The steam siren, with a pressure of 160 lbs per sq inch, has been erected at the power station instead of the steam whistle, & there was a successful trial on Tuesday morning. This will give warnings to residents in the Kingsgate, Northdown & Reading Street areas.

WAR INDUSTRY May 1st
Since its conception last August, the local shirt making industry for the troops has produced over 5,000 shirts.

In an attempt to scotch local rumours, the "Mail" reported
GERMAN PRISONERS IN THANET? May 15th

German Prisoners of War are now interned in Ramsgate & Margate. 80 German Officers & 25 other ranks are now at Margate, & a similar number at Ramsgate, & have been there for about a month. There are a number of Barons & Counts among them, & it can be accepted as definite that there are other German Officers in English places which are subject to aerial bombardment.

The Margate prisoners are at Margate College & are employed as cooks & tailors, & in the sanitary upkeep of the establishment. No expense has been incurred on their quarters. There are no dugouts in the gardens, & the prisoners are not allowed to walk the promenade.

MILITARY TRIBUNAL

At Saturdays Military Tribunal, (May 22nd) at Canterbury, the Chief Clerk of the Isle of Thanet Tramway & Electric Light Company, aged 42, appealed against enlistment. The company stated that the man was the only one who could work out & keep up to date the innumerate Government returns required today. No one else has the technical knowledge to do the job.

Lord Harris for the Tribunal said, "I fancy the Government departments may have to learn to do without a great many statuary forms from now on. Appeal dismissed".

BIG ST PETERS BLAZE May 21st

Damage amounting to £2,500 was caused this morning at the Tramway Depot at St Peters. Mr Gifford, a motor bus driver, employed by the company, noticed flames issuing from the store room & raised the alarm at around 8.30am.

The Broadstairs & St Peters Volunteer Fire Brigade was summonsed, the men hurrying from as far away as Ramsgate.

Delay was caused however by the tardy arrival of the horses. & when the manual, (fire engine), reached the scene of the fire, it had a good hold, being fanned by a stiff north easterly wind, & quickly spread to the mess road.

Meantime a number of men engaged at the time, entered the store, & were successful in saving a quantity of tickets & return sheets.

The arrival of the Broadstairs manual was quickly followed by the Margate motor fire engine, & with a number of employees & other volunteers, who were attracted to the scene, were, however poorly supplied with water from the Magdala Road hydrant. Had it not been for the good supply at the depot reservoir drawn upon by the Margate motor, the consequences would probably have been more serious.

It took about an hour's hard work in putting out the flames, & by then both buildings had been practically gutted. Nevertheless they were instrumental in preventing the flames spreading to the electrical generating buildings.

This conflagration will no doubt once more draw public attention to the inadequacies of the Broadstairs appliance, & another demand will be made for improvements.

The "Mail" defended the use of the word "tardy" with relationship to the above fire. Much criticism has been raised over our use of the word "tardy" in last weeks fire report. The horses for the Broadstairs manual had to come from the Pierremont stable to the fire station at the Broadway, & it is claimed it took 10 minutes to hitch them to the engine, from the time that the fire alarm sounded. "What damage could be done in that time?" we ask. The question of the horses is only a side issue, & the word "tardy" was not meant as a derogatory word aimed at the men, only at the equipment.

FOOD FROM THE SEA June 5th

Arrangements have now been made whereby residents of Broadstairs & St Peters can purchase fresh local fish at a cheaper rate than elsewhere.

The local Authority has opened a "market" for fresh fish at controlled prices, which will come under the Food Control Committee.

The Council have entered into an agreement with Mr Hiller, the only commercial fisherman at present operating in the town, to purchase his total catches. Mr F Watling, of Albion Street, has been appointed retailer, with the fish not being sold for more that 10% above his purchase price.

The use of the fresh fish shop, "Uncle Toms Cabin", adjacent to the Droit office, which is Council property, will be used as the retail outlet.

Customers will have to supply their own paper or receptacle, & if there is any doubt as to their residency, a food card will have to be produced.

The fish is to be sold in the evenings, & the use of the "war telegram" boards will announce the times of the opening of the "market" each day. This will also be relayed to Mr Wards Chemists, at St Peters.

The first catch on Monday was small, being only 8 stone of fish, due to a north easter blowing, but ready purchasers were eagerly waiting at the pier head for the trawlers arrival, & within the hour all of the catch had been sold.

Over the next 5 days, the catches were averaging 16 stone per day. .

APPOINTMENTS

Councillor H Bing has been appointed Head Special Constable for Broadstairs & St Peters. (May 29th)

Dr Brightman, the Council Chairman, has been made a Major in No 5 Field Ambulance R A M C. (June 12th)

Mr Dan Mason has accepted the Presidency of the newly formed Allotment Holders Association. (June 12th)

On June 26th the gas went up another 6d per 1,000 cu feet.

Bowling is now in full swing on the immaculate bowling greens in Pierremont pleasure grounds. These are open to both visitors & residents alike.

The Bowling Club has been suspended until more rosy days.

FEMALE CHAIR ATTENDANT

The Broadstairs Entertainments Committee are keeping abreast of the times by appointing the first lady chair attendant in Thanet. It is appropriate that Mrs Bax, whose husband Mr Bax, carried out the duties before the war, has been engaged. Mr Bax is now engaged in work of National importance at Woolwich.

FATAL FLYING ACCIDENT July 3rd

Apparently falling into an "air pocket", whilst at a low altitude, near to the monument, (Whitfield Tower) at Northdown at noon on Monday, a double seater bi-plane, piloted by Flight Sergeant Felton of the R A F, nose dived & crashed. Sergeant Felton was the only occupant & sadly died in the crash.

The Rev C H S Matthews Vicar of St Peters, has changed his surplus for khaki & has received orders to be ready for embarkation on the 16th July.

BRIGHTER DAYS July 10th

Brighter days at last appear to be at hand for Broadstairs & St Peters, for during the past week or two, a steady influx of visitors has been the order. In addition quite a large number of former residents have returned.

The free & easy attitude of the visitors in the streets & along the front & beach has helped to reproduce, to a slight extent, the pre-war appearance of the town, & material assistance has been given by the efforts of the Entertainments Committee.

The initiative which has led to the engagement of the Royal Marines Band from Chatham, has wholeheartedly been approved over the last weekend.

CAPTURED AT SEA

Since the inauguration of the fish "market" on June 3rd, the following quantities of fish have been landed at the pier head, Plaice 140 stone, soles 316 lbs, skate 50 stone, plus several lobsters. A second boat is expected to proceed to the fishing grounds within the next few days.

Broadstairs Food Committee is prepared to release a quantity of sugar upon the insistence that it is for use only as a preservative, i.e. for the making of jams.

BATHING FACILITIES July 24th

Much to the surprise of many, a number of bathing machines made their appearance on the sands on Monday. With the additional number of cabins & tents recently erected, the hope had been expressed that the machines were a thing of the past. In the pre-war season, valuable space in the bay was appropriated by these machines, & with the steady influx of visitors, it is hoped that the authorities will limit the number of machines to as few as possible.

It is cheering news, which comes from the Clerk of the Council, that although he is not exactly "snowed under", he has numerous applicants daily writing to him for particulars as to rooms & accommodation, & he has requested all boarding & apartment houses who have vacancies to get in touch with him.

On July 31st, the decision was arrived at to open the Town Yard as a depot for the collection of fruit stones & nut shells, which are required by the National Salvage Council. These are to be used for the production of charcoal, which is used in connection with gas masks for the men at the Front. Assistance is requested from all the Elementary Schools in the town.

(This also explains why the Girl Guides were collecting horse chestnuts last autumn)

AUGUST BANK HOLIDAY Aug 7th

After last years very quiet August Bank Holiday, this year has passed all expectations.

The following numbers of people arrived at the railway station over the week, Monday 240, Tuesday 198, Wednesday 279, Thursday 296, Friday 393, Saturday 594, Sunday morning 280, a total of 2,280 extra people.

> **BROADSTAIRS & ST. PETER'S ENTERTAINMENTS COMMITTEE.**
>
> Through the efforts of a Private Gentleman,
>
> **A WEEK - END BAND**
>
> WILL BE ENGAGED FOR
>
> **JULY & AUGUST** (including Bank Holiday).
>
> For this purpose Subscriptions are now asked, and may be sent to Mr. J. STOCKLEY, York Cottage, Broadstairs.

The Entertainment Committee had arranged a fine series of band concerts at the bandstand, their holiday programme started on Thursday, with the famous 25th (Red Horse Shoe) Division, straight from the Western Front, who gave delightful concerts in the afternoon & evenings. Long before playing time at both performances every deckchair. & shelter seat was appropriated. In addition hundreds of folk found standing room on the periphery. It is estimated that nearly 2,000 chair tickets were issued, 800 in the afternoon, & 1,100 in the evening.

From early in the morning until late in the afternoon the sea was dotted with bathers, & at times there were queues to the bathing cabins. The old pier, which asserts itself darkly emphatic upon a green bed of sea, has another attraction in the form of the "Lusitania" Life Raft, which is a reminder of the many atrocities perpetrated by the Germans.

Performances by H M Royal Marines Orchestral Band were well patronised on Sunday.

PROPOSED PUBLIC KITCHEN Aug 21st

A desire has been expressed for the establishment in Broadstairs & St Peters of a public kitchen, such as has been set up in other places. A committee has been formed consisting of Mrs Gladstone, Mrs Wood, Miss Clowes, Miss Eveling, Miss Holt, Miss Wickham, the Rector & Mrs Robson being the Hon Secs.

Considerable information has been gathered from the experiences of other successfully run ventures. The proposed kitchen is not to be a restaurant at which meals will be served for consumption on the premises, but as an establishment where meals, or portions of meals, are prepared & cooked & will be purchased for consumption at home. The advantages are that food can be purchased & prepared more economically in bulk than in small quantities, fuel at home can be saved with much cooking being avoided, & a greater variety of food can be made possible. It is the small householder more especially who will benefit, for instance, the small householder finds it impossible to obtain a joint of meat these days, but any individual will be able to purchase a cooked joint from the kitchen. The proposal is not in any sense of a charitable nature, so it must be totally self supporting.

Money must be found for the preliminary expenses, & it is hoped that all the money can be repaid over the weeks of operation. A subscription fund has been started & it is estimated that a sum of £150 will be required.

Over the next few months the money & suitable premises at No 6 the Broadway were found. The Public Kitchens were opened by Mr Norman Craig M P on December 3rd.

THE FISH MARKET AS AN ATTRACTION Aug 28th

Amongst this seasons new attraction at Broadstairs must be included the wartime fish market.

Those who are sceptical will find a visit well worth while. As an attraction of a public utility it is proving its value more & more each day.

There are now two trawlers in daily operation to the fishing grounds, the new vessel only being launched on the 19th, (August).

Our representative visited on a day when 128 stones of fish were brought ashore. Long before selling time had arrived, Harbour Street was thronged with would be purchasers; included in the crowd were many visitors, all eager to get a chance of some "food from the sea".

Weighing was speedily accomplished & Mr Watling was soon hard at work. When selling he has the assistance of Mr Nash, the Harbour Master Mr Pettit, & his assistant. An improvement in regulating the rush of buyers was noticed for in addition to "Uncle Toms Cabin", the adjoining shop has also been utilised as the entrance. At intervals 12 customers were passed through & on purchasing were passed out of another exit, keeping a clear passageway for those waiting to be served.

During the selling time some amusing incidents occurred, some having forgotten their wrapping paper, & devised various receptacles such as the kiddies sand bucket, beach towels etc, one lady even used her bathing cap. No favouritism was noticed.

On Monday the most popular fish were small plaice at 6d/lb whilst medium place were 10d/lb. Soles & skate were also in demand. In just over an hour 250 customers had been served, all leaving with radiant smiles.

The catches of late have been good, & upward of 850 stones have been disposed of since the scheme was inaugurated.

The boatmen are Mssrs S & W Hiller & J & E Croom, with Mr Stevenson is their mechanic. They spend an average of 10 hours a day at the fishing grounds, which are up to 16 miles away.

Since Dan Mason had Purchased Pierremont Hall in July 1917, many people were wondering what he was going to do with it. He had already stated that he was not going to live in as he was quite happy at The "Maisonette". Over the summer of 1918, he used it as a base for raising funds for his favourite charity, St Dunstan's Home for Blind Soldiers.

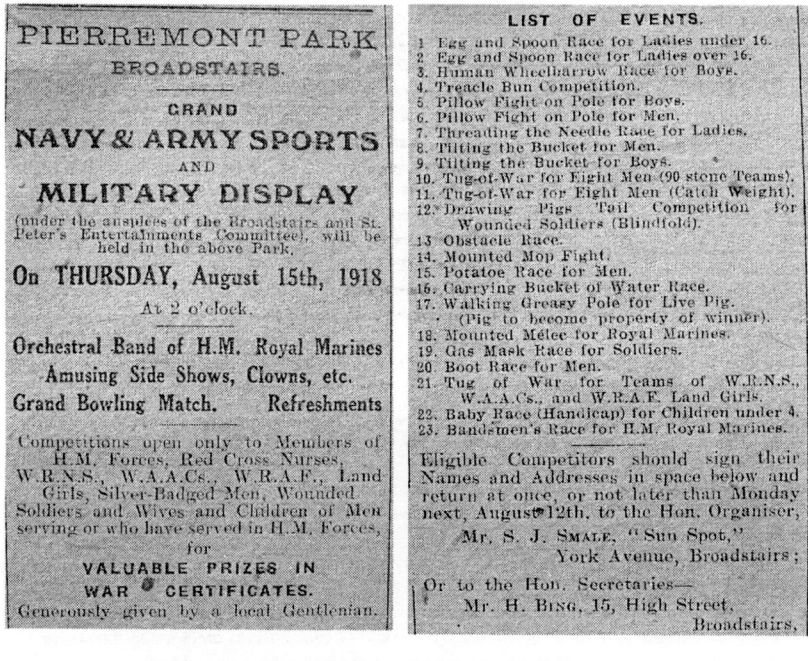

PIERREMONT PARK
BROADSTAIRS.

GRAND
NAVY & ARMY SPORTS
AND
MILITARY DISPLAY

(under the auspices of the Broadstairs and St. Peter's Entertainments Committee), will be held in the above Park,

On THURSDAY, August 15th, 1918

At 2 o'clock.

Orchestral Band of H.M. Royal Marines
Amusing Side Shows, Clowns, etc.
Grand Bowling Match.   Refreshments

Competitions open only to Members of H.M. Forces, Red Cross Nurses, W.R.N.S., W.A.A.Cs., W.R.A.F., Land Girls, Silver-Badged Men, Wounded Soldiers and Wives and Children of Men serving or who have served in H.M. Forces, for

VALUABLE PRIZES IN WAR CERTIFICATES.

Generously given by a local Gentleman.

LIST OF EVENTS.
1. Egg and Spoon Race for Ladies under 16.
2. Egg and Spoon Race for Ladies over 16.
3. Human Wheelbarrow Race for Boys.
4. Treacle Bun Competition.
5. Pillow Fight on Pole for Boys.
6. Pillow Fight on Pole for Men.
7. Threading the Needle Race for Ladies.
8. Tilting the Bucket for Men.
9. Tilting the Bucket for Boys.
10. Tug-of-War for Eight Men (90 stone Teams).
11. Tug-of-War for Eight Men (Catch Weight).
12. Drawing Pigs Tail Competition for Wounded Soldiers (Blindfold).
13. Obstacle Race.
14. Mounted Mop Fight.
15. Potatoe Race for Men.
16. Carrying Bucket of Water Race.
17. Walking Greasy Pole for Live Pig. (Pig to become property of winner).
18. Mounted Mélee for Royal Marines.
19. Gas Mask Race for Soldiers.
20. Boot Race for Men.
21. Tug of War for Teams of W.R.N.S., W.A.A.Cs., and W.R.A.F. Land Girls.
22. Baby Race (Handicap) for Children under 4.
23. Bandsmen's Race for H.M. Royal Marines.

Eligible Competitors should sign their Names and Addresses in space below and return at once, or not later than Monday next, August 12th, to the Hon. Organiser,

Mr. S. J. SMALE, "Sun Spot,"
York Avenue, Broadstairs;

Or to the Hon. Secretaries—
Mr. H. BING, 15, High Street,
Broadstairs.

THE FUTURE OF PIERREMONT HALL Aug 28th

Since a well known local gentleman has purchased Pierremont Hall some months ago, suggestions have been rife as to the probable use to which the fine old residence was to be put.

Today we are able to make a definite authentic statement on the matter. The building will be used as a social club, & preparations are now in hand for the opening.

The club will be non-political & non-sectarian in character, & will be opened for the residents of Broadstairs & St Peters on October 3rd.

The membership will be limited, so that as the men who have been fighting return home, there will be vacancies available for them. No one under 18 will be accepted. Subscriptions have been fixed at 6d per month, & the owner reserves the right to refuse membership.

Rooms will be set aside for members only at a nominal fee. It is proposed to hold entertainments, lectures etc, from time to time, & if successful it is proposed to add a library, a billiard room, & refreshment rooms. If there are insufficient applications for membership by the end of September, then the project will not be proceeded with.

The primary object of the owner is to encourage & give residents an opportunity of mutual intercourse. All credit & general thanks are due to him for his efforts in endeavouring to fulfil a popular desire.

The club grounds will be thrown open to the public on October 1st on behalf of St Dunstan's Home for Blind Soldiers.

Grand AL-FRESCO BALL
at 7 o'clock.

It is earnestly wished that the residents of the town will co-operate with the Committee to make the Fete a huge success by a display of Flags and Bunting on the day.

Remember, this is an occasion on which all can help to the happiness of our Boys on Active Service, and the Wives and Families and their Relatives awaiting their return.

TICKETS now obtainable from Members of the Committee. Adults 8d., and Children 4d. (including tax).

Trams stop at both entrances of the Park.

PLEASE NOTE.—If the weather is unfavourable, postponed until Thursday, August 22nd.

COME AND SEE
HOW BROADSTAIRS IS HELPING TO WIN THIS WAR.

GRAND SHOW
OF
Vegetables, Fruit and Utility Rabbits,
IN
PIERREMONT HALL GROUNDS
ON
Thursday, August 29th,
At 2.30 p.m. Admission 6d.

SALE by AUCTION of RABBITS
At 6 p.m.

THE PIERREMONT CLUB
Mr Dan Mason answers some questions & suggestions.

The following letter is from Mr Dan Mason of the "Maisonette" Broadstairs, in reference to the suggested use of Pierremont Hall.

He says, "Many have been the suggested use of the Hall since I purchased the buildings, especially since the last St Dunstan's Week, & I have been asked when it will be opened to the blind soldiers.

As great as my sympathies are for those who have lost their all, I feel that to place them in the centre of Broadstairs would be a great trial to many residents, also it might be a means of keeping the visitors away.

Some have said that these thoughts should not influence me, but putting these aside, it is necessary for the blind soldiers to live in a place where they can learn different trades, also poultry farming, & gardening etc. I believe that Dickens House in Hastings is well geared up for this, & will do the job admirably, & they will not be as noticeable for their walks amongst such a large population.

Others have suggested a town hall, but the building is totally unsuitable for this. With so many small rooms there would be absolutely no proper supervision, & a great deal of inefficiency, & it would make a poor makeshift for the same. If residents require a town hall, they could, for very little more money, erect an up to date building, with offices all on one floor. The latter could all be let out, & probably pay for the rest of the building.

I have decided that Pierremont Hall should be for the use of Broadstairs & St Peters residents & for our boys when they return home from the Front.

Many have said that the idea is doomed to fail, that I do not know, Broadstairs. Those who wish to join the Social Club are asked to attend on October 10th".

Over 200 enrolled within the first month, & the Pierremont Social Club held its first night on 20th November 1918. The Club survived successfully at Pierremont until 1922.

INDECENT BATHERS Sept 4th

The growing practice of certain persons at Broadstairs in proceeding to the shore, from their house or temporary accommodation, clad in a bathing costume & with a mackintosh as their only means of covering is to be stopped.

Discussions relevant to the complaint took place at the Council meeting on Monday. Reading a letter which referred to one lady & gentleman, who allegedly made it a regular practice of bathing without a machine or tent, & walking through the streets to the shore & back again with only a mackintosh covering their bathing costumes, "which is strictly against bye-law regulations on two counts", expressed the Clerk.

"It was not decent for people to walk the streets in just bathing costumes", said Cllr Nash. Cllr Bing said, it was a growing problem, & for standards of decency, must be stopped at once.

The two people in question were warned by correspondence that they must abide by the regulations.

The Clerk also reported that his application to the Local Government Board had produced 1,500 sandbags which were now in the town yard, & were to be used at dugout shelters.

New ration books were to be introduced on September 11th.

INTERNATIONAL STORES

QUALITY PRICE SERVICE

NEW RATION BOOKS

Now is the time to change your supplier if you wish to do so. You must apply to your Local Food Committee immediately, and must be able to give some satisfactory reason for so doing.

If you do change, we offer our best services if you

NOMINATE US

INTERNATIONAL STORES
TEA GROCERIES PROVISIONS

BROADSTAIRS & ST. PETER'S LOCAL FOOD CONTROL COMMITTEE.

NEW RATION BOOKS.

NOTICE IS HEREBY GIVEN that all persons holding Ration Books issued from the under-mentioned Office, must deliver up to the Food Office, Council Offices, Broadstairs, either personally or by post, NOT LATER THAN WEDNESDAY, the 18th SEPTEMBER INSTANT, the Green Slip headed "Reference Leaf" No. Y/6 or the green slip referred to may be deposited by the holder thereof with either of the Retailers mentioned on the inside of the cover of the Ration Book.

All holders of Ration Books are particularly requested properly to fill up the declaration marked "For use after October 1st only," on the bottom half of such Reference Leaf.

NOTICE is hereby further given that if the Reference Leaf above-mentioned is not handed to the Food Office or Retailer by the date named, a NEW RATION BOOK WILL NOT BE ISSUED.

L. A. SKINNER,
Executive Officer.

Food Office, Council Offices, Broadstairs.
7th September, 1918.

By November 6th the shirt making industry at Broadstairs had produced 8,200 shirts, & more workers were required to boost production up to 100 shirts a week.

The Little Comforts Association was still in business & was still sending 21 parcels out each week. The Little League at St Peters was also still in operation, but was by this time down to 15 parcels a week, due mainly to a lack of funds.

In helping to relieve the coal shortage, we learn that many lady residents are resorting to the use of the hay box for cooking. Much fuel, according to one enthusiast, is saved, whilst the dish requires no attention whilst in the box, & cannot be overcooked, as well as the nourishing value of the food is not impaired.

THE END OF THE FIGHTING Nov 13th
RAMSGATE GETS THE NEWS BEFORE LONDON
CELEBRATIONS BEGIN AT ONCE-A MEMORABLE DAY

A perfectly golden dawn on Monday (11th), which bathed the whole horizon with a red glow, ushered in a day of thanksgiving & rejoicing at Ramsgate, equal to none in the history of the town.

There was a feeling of tension as people began to prepare for business. They little knew it, but at the same time there was being wafted across the Downs, a message by wireless saying, that the armistice with Germany had been signed, & that fighting was to cease at 11am, - a message to make the whole of the Allied countries hilarious.

Apparently "picked up" at Dover, it was transmitted to Ramsgate as a naval base, & at precisely 9.45am, those aboard the drifters or patrol boats in the harbour received it. And with them lay the honour of conveying it to the townsfolk at large.

There was no hesitation! The skippers, or the nearest man, jumped for the siren rope, & soon there arose a screeching & succession of long drawn out blasts, which would have awakened the dead. Ramsgate had deserved the honour of being the first town on the coast to get the news. Even London did not get it until one hour later.

And then the party started, shops & offices closed, bunting went up, the Mayor shut his business & joined the happy throng. Telegrams to the King & appropriate war leaders were all sent & celebrations went on into the early hours of the following morning. Meanwhile at Broadstairs………..

The news was not received at Broadstairs until sometime later, although the hooting of the drifters at Ramsgate could be plainly heard.

Many people made tracks for the Council Offices, to see if any official announcement had been exhibited, whilst others rang up their friends at Ramsgate to hear of any definite news. Later, rumours gained currency that the message had been picked up by wireless earlier that morning. A rush was made at once to purchase flags & bunting, & within a short space of time, all the local supplies had been "snapped up". Others, anticipating a joyful day, had already secured their peace trophies, & were quickly at work exhibiting them in the most prominent positions. The news soon spread, & within a short space of time the town presented an animated scene. Union Jacks were flying from the most prominent buildings in the town, while streamers of flags of the Allies were suspended across the main thoroughfares. Others gave prominence to shields bearing the royal arms & patriotic mottos. At 10.45 the sirens in the High Street, Rumfields water works, & the power station began to sound the confirmation of the happy news.

Considering its importance, many were expecting a public announcement from the Council Offices, but they were disappointed, as none came. The official news was despatched from London at 10.52, & finally reached Broadstairs at 12.30, when it was at once exhibited on the war telegram boards at the Council Offices & around the town.

The houses of business were closed from 12 o'clock, each celebrated as they thought best. No manifestations had been organised by the "powers that be", with the exception of a Thanksgiving Service at the bandstand in the afternoon.

The good news was told to the sick & wounded at "Fairfield" V A D Hospital by one of the sisters with the words, "They've signed boys, they've signed". Excitement & enthusiasm reigned for some time.

The convalescent & sick men at the V A D Hospital "Roseneath", received the news with jubilation & rejoicing.

The scholars at the Broadstairs Boys School were told of the glad tidings by their headmaster, Mr T O Studd, where they all sang the National Anthem, & were promptly dismissed for the day.

An appropriate placard, bearing the letters "R I P" was hung on the High Street siren.

Soon after the news, a unit of the Yorkshire Regiment passed through the town, having left Margate on a route march. Cheers were given as they marched through the streets. The soldiers at the "Oaklands" School of Signals in St Peters, were soon on parade. In the cap of each was flying a miniature Union Jack, as they proceeded to the sea promenade from the village, rendering choruses of popular songs as they went.

A special thanksgiving service was held in the evening at St Peters Church, at which the Rev Mark Cassidy gave an appropriate address.

No public announcement was made until the evening, when Dr Brightman, the Chairman of the Council, spoke to the audience at the Cinema.

The following scathing letter appeared in the "Mail" on November 20th.

RESIDENTS COMPLAINT REGARDING ARMISTICE DAY ARRANGEMENTS

The lamentable lack of organised rejoicing at Broadstairs, at the signing of the Armistice with Germany & the cessation of hostilities on Monday 11th, has called forth the appended letter, signed "A B C", one resident writes,

"Regret has been freely expressed that Broadstairs did not rise to the occasion as they did in other towns. I think it is very unfair to blame the residents for the lack of enthusiasm on the day.

We looked at usual to the local Council to make suitable arrangements, but they failed to realise the significance & the meaning of the armistice, & they are in consequence, the culprits & stand impeached.

On the eventful morning, everyone, with the exemption of the Council, felt something tremendous was about to take place. Suppressed excitement was on every face, a silent note of buoyancy & liveliness were plainly evident, in fact it was extremely difficult to "carry on" as usual, and this is how the day was observed a Broadstairs.

Early on Monday morning, at around 9.45, enquiries were made at the Council Offices for official news, were the sirens to be sounded, & so on. The answer given, "We know nothing & we are too busy to bother about it", -Ye Gods! May I say in passing, that the Council during the whole of the bad old years, the policy of laissez-faire – to let things alone & take their course. We have not forgotten how difficult it was to get the Council to "move on" in connection with the provision of the dugouts, which would have kept many more people in the town.

Whilst the people of Ramsgate & Margate were giving true expression of their feelings, we had to wait until later in the day before the local "powers that be" condescended to enlighten us.

At 3 o'clock we wended our way to the bandstand, & fully expecting "something good". The result was a one sided show, principally designed for a section of the inhabitants, those belonging to the state-church, other denominations were given the cold shoulder, how different it was in Ramsgate where all were given the same opportunity.

And this concluded the Official Programme of the Council, & many expressions of disgust naturally followed. Crowds went to Ramsgate, where the joyful celebrations were in full progress.

In the meantime, the local "powers that be", must have got the "wind up", for we find the Chairman of the Council at the Cinema in the evening. He told us, "He didn't consider it a day for rejoicing", (even the little children knew differently). & that the Council would not be behind when Peace Day arrived. This attempt at an apology did not find much favour".

Another correspondent described the Thanksgiving Service at the bandstand as "Ecclesiastical Kaiserism".

After the celebrations died away, the town then had to re-adjust to rapid changes. The first thing to get stood down was the Home Front Volunteers on November 13th. The Government decided to stop all recruiting under the Military Service Act, & the Military Tribunals were suspended. Though the fighting had stopped, residents were reminded that rationing on certain foods was still in place, & the lighting & heating regulations were still in force. It was no longer necessary to keep the curtains closed, but the numbers of lights showing in the towns were to be kept to a minimum to conserve fuel. There was a local influenza epidemic, with as many as five people dying in St Peters in one week. The Sunday performances at the Cinema were suspended, & gradually the V A D hospitals were emptied of patients.

FAREWELL TO TROOPS November 27th

A big concert took place at the Y M C A "Albion Hut" on Wednesday evening. The interior of the building was elaborately decorated for the occasion. An evening of musical merriment, & laughter followed, where friendships were terminated, & promises were made. The evening fittingly ended with signing of "Auld Lang Syne", & the National Anthem.

The "Albion Hut" was closed down on 11th December & by then all the troops had been withdrawn from the town.

On December 4th, the Y M C A Authorities offered the wooden sides of the "Drill Hall" at Crampton Tower to the Council for £144 10s, which was referred to the Council General Purposes Committee.

Roseneath was opened in October 1914, & closed on 21st Feb 1918. Over this period, Roseneath & Fairfield Hospitals treated a total of 2,159 servicemen, mainly from overseas, tending their wounds & nursing them back to health.

Roseneath V A D Hospital St Peters Park Road.

Members of The Queens (West Surry Regiment), relax over a game of billiards at the YMCA "Albion Hut", in the disused gas works in Albion Street. The "Hut" closed on 11th December 1918.

WAR WORKERS RELAX

    At the Cinema on Friday evening, a relaxing evening was given by the Council to all those who had undertaken voluntary war work. The hall was packed with servicemen, nurses from the V A D hospitals, Red Cross nurses, land girls, Girl Guides, Y M C A workers, V A D men, firemen, special constables, the Buffs Volunteers, the Kent Field Ambulance plus all their friends & guests. Most turned up in their respective uniforms, those of the Red Cross nurses & land girls standing out bold to that of sombrous khaki.

    Major Brightman took the chair, & explained that the evening would be totally informal, & those present should have a totally happy & enjoyable evening.

    Most of the entertainment in the form of songs both patriotic & comic, monologues, ventriloquism, or artistic sketches, came from those attending the event.

On December 4th, the first post-war proposal for a dugout was put to the Council. This was for the dugout that ran from the Waterloo Steps under the promenade to approximately the Albion Steps.

A SCENIC RAILWAY

The sands dugout at Broadstairs is likely to be put to a novel, & what may possibly prove to be, an attractive use in the future.

At a meeting of the Council last week, a letter was read out by the Clerk submitting a scheme for the construction of a scenic railway. Expressing an opinion that this proposal would be an attraction, & a source of revenue for the town, the writer mentioned that the passages would have to be enlarged in both width & height. At various distances scenes representing the industries of the colonies would be arranged, & the recesses containing them would be illuminated with coloured electric lighting. There would also be copies of Bairnsfather's pictures in figures, & at one end a miniature jungle. The plans had already been prepared by a qualified architect, & an electrical engineer.

The existing entrance at Waterloo Stairs would be filled in & an entranceway made from the main Albion Steps. He would be prepared to accept a lease of 7, 14, or 21 years rated at £30, £40, or £50 respectively. Mr Wilson concluded his letter by mentioning that he had been a contractor on the sands, (tents), for the last 18 years, & if the proposal were found to be favourable, he did not intend for the attraction to be open on Sundays.

The idea was turned down flat by the Council. This was followed by a letter one week later asking if the Council also proposed to put a steam operated roundabout in Nuckells Gardens.

Bruce Bairnsfather Cartoon

By the end of December the Prisoners of War started returning home with much family rejoicing. With them came the stories of the suffering that they had endured whilst carrying out enforced labour for the Germans. Social gatherings were held at all the public venues in the town to welcome the demobilised & prisoners back home.

1919

At the Council meeting of January 8th, the Council attempted to put a priority list together of work that had to be done. High on the list was the town lighting, which had suffered with neglect over the previous three years. Most had fallen apart through lack of use & a lack of maintenance. Virtually all the gas mantles in the gas lights had disappeared. Roads were another priority since having taken over the responsibility of Westwood, Northwood, & Kingsgate back in 1913, very little had been done owing to the war. The roads were described as being *"in a deplorable condition"* & an estimate of between £40,000 & £50,000 was thought necessary to put the infrastructure into some kind of order.

Permission was asked for by the Aviation Co Ltd, to fly their four seater biplanes from the foreshore for pleasure trips, & could the Council find them a suitable site for a hanger. This was turned down as *"Broadstairs is quite unsuitable for this kind of venture"*. The Aviation Co then tried its luck at Ramsgate, but was also turned down.

A letter was read out at the meeting, asking the Council whether they were prepared to consider making the baths behind the Council Offices, available to the general public now the military weren't using them.

The breakwater on the north side of the pier, for the unloading of the fishing boats at low water was started, and once again the question of the seafront concert hall, something that had vexed the Council for some 20 years, was put back on the agenda.

On January 15th, the "shirt making industry" finally closed down, & at the end of the month "Fairfield" V A D Hospital finally closed. All the remaining patients were transferred to "Roseneath", which shut at the end of February. Since "Fairfield" & "Roseneath" had been occupied by the V A D as a hospital, 2,159 servicemen, mainly from overseas, had been nursed back to health.

FORESHORE FINDS Feb 12th

Novel scenes were witnessed on the foreshore at Dumpton during the weekend, when the poorer residents of both Ramsgate & Broadstairs found a visit to the rocks & sands most profitable.

From the wreck of the American steamer "Piave", which was wrecked on the Goodwins on January 29th, was washed ashore a considerable quantity of cargo, comprising in the most part of sacks of fine white flour.

Despite their immersion, it was found that when they were opened, that the water had had the effect of effectively sealing the centre, with the result that those who cared to take the trouble, could carry away one or two bushels of good dry flour from each sack. All kinds of receptacles were utilised to remove the spoils home, boxes on wheels, pillow cases, handkerchiefs, & even aprons were brought into use. The primitive methods adopted meant the recipients, mainly children, were seen tramping home with the appearance of millers.

A number of barrels of lard were also found "stranded", & were removed home by the "early birds".

As the men were gradually being demobbed, their businesses re-opened & the town took on a resemblance of early 1914. A batch of children arrived at the Metropolitan Convalescent Home in Lanthorne Road on February 19th, & was soon followed by the girls from the Tait Homes in April.

On March 12th, the last 53 parcels were sent out to St Peters men still serving by the Little Comforts Fund. A total of over 3,000 packages had been sent since the formation of the organisation in 1916, & a total of £420 had been raised & expended.

RE-OPENING.

W. L. NASH

Begs to inform the Inhabitants that he is REOPENING HIS BUSINESS on

SATURDAY, MARCH 15th.

He regrets owing to illness he will not be able to give his personal attention for a few weeks. But arrangements have been made that Customers shall have the best value at lowest prices, and he trusts he will renew the confidence always placed in him in the past.

7, HIGH STREET,
BROADSTAIRS.

March, 1919.

DEMOBILIZED.

F. C. WILKS,

WATCHMAKER AND JEWELLER,

HARBOUR STREET, Broadstairs,

HAS now Re-opened his Business after serving with the Colours abroad. High-class repairs to all watches, clocks and jewellery. All work done on the premises. Personal attention. Best prices given for old gold and silver, works of art, and antique furniture.

A TRIAL SOLICITED.

HAVE YOUR KHAKI DYED!

There is good cloth in your Army clothes. Why not let us dye them for civilian wear?

Officers' Tunics, Trousers and Overcoats Dyed, and alterations carried out.

Privates' Overcoats dyed Brown or Blue, from 12/6, which will give you better service than one costing four to six guineas.

CLEANING and DYEING OF ALL MEN'S WEAR.

ACHILLE SERRE, Ltd.,
4, Ramsgate Road, Broadstairs.

By the end of May, sufficient numbers of schoolteachers had been demobbed, to enable the schools in the town to re-start at the beginning of the Easter term.

St Peters Court. Wellesley House, Hildersham, Bartrum Gables, Abbotsford, Rimpton, St Georges, Dumpton House, Selwyn House, & Brondsbury schools were all back in full operation.

At the end of the Council year in April, Dr Brightman, who had been Chairman of the Council throughout the first war, stood down & declined re-election as a Councillor.
COUNCIL WORK ENDED   DR BRIGHTMAN'S VALEDICTORY.

At Wednesday night's council meeting, Dr Brightman took his place for the last time at the conclusion of the ordinary business of the Council meeting. He gave a resume of the work carried out by the Council over the war time period.
During the course of his speech, he said that as a Council they had not made much progress, but had managed to keep the town going, & judging from the position they were now in, had kept it going successfully.
One of the most anxious times he had, was in February 1917, the time when the volunteers & troops were called out in the neighbourhood. About 5 o'clock in the afternoon he was sitting at his home, Apsley House, when the code word came through, telling him to prepare Broadstairs for evacuation.
"I can assure you that it was the most worrying half hour of my life", said Dr Brightman. He was allowed to consult with scarcely anyone, but he saw the Chief Constable, & Councillor Hicks. They put their

heads together, but they had a very anxious time indeed. "Fortunately the order to stand down was received before the ball actually got rolling".

Another anxious period was March 1918, when the Germans made their serious push, & it looked as though they would get to the channel coast.

Broadstairs & St Peters Mail 16th April 1919.

"IN CASE", THE THANET EVACUATION SCHEME 25th April 1919

Now that Censorship of the Press is somewhat relieved we are permitted to publish the full particulars of the elaborate preparations made by the local authorities for the evacuation of the Thanet towns in the event of the danger of an invasion of our coast becoming acute.

Unfortunately perhaps from one point of view, we were not allowed to more than hint at these preparations during the times of danger, but the details, now that the dark days are over, make interesting reading.

BROADSTAIRS & THE RURAL DISTRICT

A most comprehensive scheme for the evacuation of the area under the Authority of the Urban District Council of Broadstairs & the Rural District Council of Thanet, was drawn up by the body which came into existence, known as the Thanet Emergency Committee. It was submitted to Lieut.-General Sir Frederick Stopford, KC,MG, on Feb 12th 1915, & was subsequently brought up to date in accordance with various instruction received.

Major Powell Cotton, of Birchington, was Chairman & military member, & with Mr L Skinner of Broadstairs, to make the arrangements as effective as possible. The members of the committee were Mr Brightman JP, (representing the Broadstairs area), Mr A W Miller, (representing the farmers & stockholders), Alderman W Booth Reeve,(representing the Margate area), the Mayor of Ramsgate, Mr R Grant, JP, (representing the Westgate area), & Major Hilton-Johnson, (representing the western side of the island).

Each town or village, appointed members of the local Council to act under the Chairman, & subcommittees were appointed as follows, Broadstairs, vehicles, horse & motor, Mr H Hicks, harbour & boats, Mr H Bing. The Broadstairs & St Peters local committee consisted of Dr Brightman, (Chairman), Messrs Byron, Bowie, Bing, A & F Foster, Moodey, Nash, Pemble, Snowden, & the Rev Ridgeway, with Mr L Skinner as Hon Sec. The police were then represented by Inspector Ford, & Head Special Constable H Hicks.

The general instructions given to the residents when evacuation was ordered were to leave the town via Westwood, & thence towards the road which runs from Star Cottage over the railway to Haine Hospital, then following the road opposite the hospital to Vincent Farm, turning sharp to the left to Pouces, proceeding straight on until the main Ramsgate- Canterbury Road was reached. Crossing that road, the refugees were to proceed to Plucks Gutter via the road passing Mill & Ivy Cottage, Way, Pinks Corner, Foxborough Lane, Tothill Street, Monkton Road & through Hoo & Monkton to Gore Street.

Special Constables were to warn & direct inhabitants & instructions were given to certain of them to carry out various duties. Cycle dealers stocks which could not be ridden away were to be rendered unfit for use, oars, rudders, & gear were to be removed from boats, & a plank started near the keel to make them useless.

Information of a landing, or attempted landing, was to be conveyed to Canterbury, & Sandwich & neighbouring towns by motor cyclists, in addition to messages by phone & wire. Motor car owners were instructed on similar lines to those at Ramsgate, with the addition that if it were found impossible to remove any car it was to be rendered useless by smashing some vital part. The surveyor was ordered to make arrangements for destroying or removing all signpost arms. Wagons & carts were detailed for the conveyance of women & children as far as possible, those not useable being rendered useless or destroyed. Motor cyclists were appointed to give warnings & another to give stowage of petrol, & bicycles in cars, & to see to destruction of flour etc.

Plucks Gutter was fixed as the immediate destination of all refugees from the outlying villages. A motor car was specially earmarked at Westgate for the removal of the bullion from the two bank branches.

A confidential circular issued to farmers & stockowners by the Thanet Emergency Committee gave detailed instructions for the course to be adopted in case of emergency. It stated that the only road available for the population would be fully used, animals were to be destroyed by being shot, the carcasses not to be bled or the entrails removed, so that they would become inedible within an hour or two. The additional advice was given, that the owners should have all their horses & live stock branded or marked,, as the central organising committee for Kent had caused it to be understood that the Government would give reasonable compensation for property destroyed by the owners under the instructions of the military, or police acting under them. No destruction was to commence until the order to that effect had been received. Wagons & heavy carts were either to be destroyed by fire, rendered useless by smashing three or four consecutive spokes in the wheels or by burning or breaking the shafts. Farm horses were to be led off to Plucks Gutter. Motor car owners were instructed to keep the petrol tanks full up. Spare tins were to be placed in the cars, which were to drive off to Canterbury via the Ramsgate, or Margate to Canterbury main roads, & assemble at the cavalry barracks. Surplus petrol was to be emptied from the tins.

In the event of the above road being menaced by the enemy, civilians leaving the towns should take to the road to Sandwich. In such circumstances those on the road to Plucks Gutter should take the Sandwich Road through Minster. If the marshes are dry, the best & shortest way to Sandwich was over the marshes from Minster to Ash, via the Red House Ferry.

Where troops or military transports are met upon any of the roads, civilians must take to the fields, & leave the road clear while they are passing.

Broadstairs & St Peters Mail 25th April 1919

KENT DEFENCE.

BROADSTAIRS & ST. PETER'S

Notice to the Civil Population in Case of Emergency.

Should it be necessary for the Civil Population to remove, those who desire to do so are to proceed by the route, via WESTWOOD and FLEET to PLUCKS GUTTER.

Conveyances will, if possible, be provided to collect and carry the aged, infirm, and young children, and those in charge of them only; all others must proceed on foot.

All children under five years old must be labelled.

IMPORTANT. The people are to bring all necessary clothing, boots, blankets, etc. to protect them from the weather, also their money and available food. All articles unnecessary for subsistence to be left behind.

The Exodus will be under the control of the Police and Special Constabulary, whose instructions must be strictly obeyed.

F. BRIGHTMAN,
Chairman of Local Emergency Committee.

COUNCIL OFFICES,
BROADSTAIRS.
January 27th, 1917.

No wonder Dr Brightman was worried!

Dr Frank Brightman had been on the local board, & then the Council since 1892. He was Chairman of the Council in 1912/1913 & then again for 1914 to 1919.

WONDERFUL BROADSTAIRS   PEACE DAY CELEBRATIONS *19th July 1919*

Residents & visitors alike agree unanimously, that Saturdays Peace celebrations at Broadstairs were all that could be desired. Wonderful scenes were witnessed throughout the day during the full programme of festivities arranged. But beyond a doubt, the picture presented on the front, will derive happy memories for many years to come.

Primarily came the festivities for the rising generation in the morning. About them, one could write columns, First of all the merry crowds of adult spectators, out to get enjoyment from the enjoyment of the youngsters, who proceeded in procession from all areas of the town, to the field in Lanthorne Road, so generously placed at the disposal of the committee. The assembly took on a delightfully festive appearance for the occasion, as the laughing infants were carried there on decorated farm wagons, of the animation of the white clad girls, & no less neatly attired boys, as perspiring & gloriously happy, they entered the grounds in the charge of their teachers. What a sight they made as they lined up in a square formation round the specially erected platform.

The Rev C F Ridgeway spoke to the children, hoping that when they recalled their memories of what was hoped to be a most memorable day, they could recall why the festivities were being held. They had the longest to live & the longest recollection of this day. It was a day of victory & a reminder of the suffering of brave men & women.

The orchestral band of H M Royal Marines, & the great choir of fresh young voices, sang the National Anthem & "God bless the Prince of Wales". Despite their eagerness to start the sports, the juveniles watched with undisguised interest, a delightful display of dancing by the pupils of Brondesbury Girls School. Uncle Mack & his minstrel troupe were in evidence later, & never did they have such an appreciative audience.

The sports races then followed, which had all the usual events from egg & spoon races, sack races, to tug of war, three legged races & hopping races. Punctually at 12.30 the children all sat down to a magnificent luncheon.

ROUND THE TOWN

The town decorations were something to enthuse about. An incentive to outdo ones neighbours in the matter of beautifying the exterior of all the dwelling houses & business premises was given by the setting aside of prizes for different categories, & no matter where one went, in any direction, a profusion of bunting, of every possible description, was to be seen. "God save the King", "Victory", & "Peace", all formed delightful arrangements, alongside National flags surrounded by laurel. A novelty to be seen outside the Dickens Tea Lounge, took the form of a model aeroplane, made by Mr A E Stannard.

WATER CARNIVAL

All roads led to the seafront in the afternoon, for the happy inspiration that part of the day, was set apart for the water carnival held in the main bay. The scene, when the proceedings commenced, was reminiscent of the old regatta days, & no happier issue can be imagined, that the revival of that one time annual event.

Only sunshine was required to crown the success of the arrangements, & we had it, in all its radiance. The carnival spirit was in the air, & vibrated over the crowds the length of the promenades, on to the sands, & onto the pier, indeed on every conceivable point that was available. Good humour radiated everywhere. The water races then started in the bay, with aquatics for everyone to participate in, both male & female. Clowns, millers & sweeps, & greasy poles all added to the delight of the crowds.

THE EVENING SCENES

The delighted crowds dispersed at the close of the water sports, but were not long in reassembling in their thousands after tea, on the front & early on in the evening the appearance of that part of the town was one of a seething mass of humanity. The appearance of the front from Louisa Bridge to Harbour Street, was a massive display of colour which has never been seen before between these two points. With multicoloured bunting everywhere, fluttering from the windows, roofs, railing & balconies of houses, from poles extending along the full length of the promenade, in fact, from every possible place where it could be displayed with effect. The war memory touch was given at the be-ribboned bandstand by the exhibition of fighting implements. A lasting tribute to the gallant dead, was there too, in the form of two large display bunches of white lilies. It was such a setting that the thousands of joymakers trooped to commence the nights festivities. Many had taken up positions on deckchairs against the railings, but so dense was the crowd, what they saw was actually nothing. Miss Daphne Godolphin & Master Bunty Neal led the dancing to the band of the Royal Marines, pirouetting couples & promenaders were mixed up in a heterogonous mass, of glorious, laughing, happy assembly, the carnival spirit embraced in the afternoon, by that time fully instilled. There was no leading one's perspiring partner to a seat at the close; it was a case of standing where one stopped until the next dance commenced. Every moment seemed to add to the numbers. Songs were sung, & the final phase of the festivities began at 9.30, with the illuminations, & a surety no prettier effect was ever seen the length & breadth of England that night. Multi coloured light blazed out at the various points visible from the front. They came into being everywhere, candles & fairy lamps were placed in all the windows of the premises overlooking the front, & the bandstand became a mass of light. All along the front stretched ropes of diamond shaped electric globes of a myriad of shades, which gleamed brightly amid the bunting. Away in the distance, there appeared to be a lured glare from successively lighted deck flares, & every now & again, from inland & over the water, the varied coloured stars from the rockets seemed to curtsy to the festive assembly. The dancing continued, until footsore & weary, but glowing with contentment, the great crowd, at 11.30 linked hands & united in singing "Auld Lang Syne" to the strains of the orchestral music. The National Anthem, sung with fervour, brought to a close a most memorable day.

 The Council Chairman, Councillor Foster, thanked all those for their efforts, which enabled Broadstairs & St Peters to have one of the happiest days that has ever been known in the town. Perfect order prevailed all day, reflecting great credit on the tact & ability shown by Inspector Ford & his men.

The Broadstairs and St. Peter's Mail.

23rd July 1919

DR BRIGHTMAN'S

ROLL OF HONOUR

1915

9th List November 1915

Dr Brightman was Broadstairs & St Peters Council Chairman throughout the Great War. On more than one occasion he tried to complete a list of all those who served in the armed forces. He was purely reliant on residents & relations sending in names, but owing to the number of residents who moved away the list is probably incomplete. Some Broadstairs men were recruited at Ramsgate & Margate, whilst others in the Rural District joined up at Broadstairs. Many men also enlisted after 1915 & do not appear on this list.

Over the period 1914 to 1915, the "Mail" published 9 different lists, & by November Dr Brightman appears to have given up accumulating names. The following list gives the rank & service on enlisting where known. Many changed their regiments, & their ship as time went on, & many were of course promoted.

Dr Brightman's intention was that the completed Roll of Honour would be on permanent display within the town. As of yet it is not known whether he achieved this.

BROADSTAIRS & ST PETERS ROLL OF HONOUR 9th List Nov 1915

ALEN L.W.	PRIVATE	ESSEX REGT
ALEXANDER F.	DRIVER	AMMUNITION COLUMN 1st INDIAN CAVALRY
AMBROSE PERCY	DRIVER	R F A
ANSLEY	PRIVATE	6th BUFFS
ARNOLD	PRIVATE	2nd BUFFS
ARNOLD E.	GUNNER	ROYAL FIELD ARTILLERY
ARNOLD JOHN	PRIVATE	
ARNOLD L.	PRIVATE	
ASHLEE T.W.	LANCE CORPORAL	2nd SOUTH STAFFORDSHIRE REG
ATKINSON A.H.	PRIVATE	4th BUFFS
ATKINSON F.J.	DRIVER	R F A (T)
ATTWELL E.	DRIVER	ARMY SERVICE CORPS
ATTWELL T	CORPORAL	2nd BUFFS
ATTWOOD J.W.	PRIVATE	ARMY VETINARY CORPS
AUSTEN GEO	PRIVATE	
AUSTEN H.	LANCE CORP	ROYAL ENGINEERS SIGNAL CORPS
AUSTEN H.S.	PRIVATE	11th HUSSARS
AUSTEN JOHN	PRIVATE	
AUSTEN P.J.	BUGLER	6th CITY OF LONDON RIFLES
AUSTIN G.	CORPORAL	ROYAL ENGINEERS
AYRES EDWARD		R E K M R
BAKER	PRIVATE	6th BUFFS
BAKER A.G.	PRIVATE	R A M C
BAKER M.	PRIVATE	BUFFS
BAKER S.G.	A B	H M S ERIN
BAKER W.	PRIVATE	7th BUFFS
BARTROP A.U.	ASSIST ENGINEER	H M S SICILIA
BASSETT GEO	GUNNER	R F A
BAX	TROOPER	SOUTH AFRICAN MOUNTED RIFLES
BAX G.	P O	H M S RONDA
BAX OSMAN	LEADING SEAMAN	H M S JUNO
BAX THEODORE	P VO	H M S LANCASTER
BEAK HY	1st CLAS P O	H M S LEDA
BEAN FRED	STOKER	H M S HAMPSHIRE
BEARD H.	PRIVATE	4 th BATT MIDDLESEX REGIMENT
BEARMAN J.H.	PRIVATE	6th DRAGOON GUARDS
BEETHAM G C	PRIVATE	3rd ARTISTS RIFLES
BEETHAM H.F.A.	PRIVATE	TRANSPORT SECT 6th BATT BUFFS
BIART C.	SIGNALMAN	ROYAL ENGINEERS
BICKMORE WILLIAM		2nd LIFE GUARDS
BING C.	A B	CHATHAM
BING E.	STOKER	H M S B OSTRICH
BING E.E.	PRIVATE	9th LANCERS
BING H.	PRIVATE	9th BUFFS
BING H.	A B	H M S FORMIDABLE
BING J.	GUNNER	R F A
BING S. LEE	LANCE CORP	1st BUFFS
BING S.C.	PRIVATE	1st BUFFS
BING SID	LEADING STOKER	H M S BUONAVENTURE
BISHOP	RIFLEMAN	POST OFFICE RIFLES
BISHOP A.	C P O	H M S LAUREL
BLACKBURN S.E	PRIVATE	R A M C
BLIGH H.	TROOPER	EAST KENT YEOMANRY
BLOY A.W.	LIEUTENANT	21st COUNTY OF LONDON BATTALLION
BLOY D.	PRIVATE	LINCOLNSHIRE REGIMENT
BOTTLE T.A.	BOMBADIER	3rd KENT BATT R F A
BOTTLE W.	GUNNER	3rd KENT BATT R F A
BOWIE	PRIVATE	FIELD ARTILLERY
BOWIE	NURSE	RED CROSS
BOWIE G.	GUNNER	6th R F A
BOWLES W.	PRIVATE	4th BUFFS
BOWYER HORACE		8th BATT ROYAL WEST SURRY REG
BOWYER KENNETH		6th EAST SURREY REGIMENT
BRENCHLEY R.	STOKER	H M S RALE
BRENCHLEY R.G.	PRIVATE	2nd BATT BUFFS
BRENCHLEY ROBERT HENRY	BLACKSMITH	H M S CRESSY
BRETT R.	DRIVER	ARMY SERVICE CORPS
BRISLEY	ENGINEER	ROYAL ENGINEERS
BRISLEY	PRIVATE	GRENADIER GUARDS
BRISLEY	PIONEER SERGEANT	1st HAMPSHIRE REGIMENT
BRISLEY ALF		1st HAMPSHIRE REGIMENT
BRISLEY LESLIE		2nd GRENADIER GUARDS
BRITTER C.	PRIVATE	6th BUFFS
BROCKMAN S.	STOKER	H M S LANCE
BROOKS A.	DESPATCH RIDER	COLDSTREAM GUARDS
BROOKS A.	TROOPER	7th SIGNAL TROOP
BROWN C	PRIVATE	K R R
BROWN P.J.	SAPPER	ROYAL ENGINEERS
BROWN T.	STOKER	H M S COLLINGWOOD
BUGDEN G.J.		H M S VENGEANCE

103

Name	Rank	Unit
BUGDEN JOHN		H M SUBMARINE C19
BUMBRIDGE H.		H M S SENTINAL
BUNCE E.C.	STOKER	6th BUFFS
BUNCE JOB	SERGEANT	
BURGESS SID	PRIVATE	A O C
BURT B.	BOMBADIER	R F A
BUSHELL A.	CORP	1st BUFFS
BUSHELL GEO	DRIVER	ARMY SERVICE CORPS
BUSHELL S.W.C.	A B	H M S INDOMITABLE
BUTT F.T.	PRIVATE	R M L I
BYNG F S	GUNNER	R F A
CAIRD D.	PRIVATE	5th BUFFS
CALL A.J.	SERGEANT	8th BUFFS
CARROLL D.C.	SERGEANT	EAST SURREY REGIMENT
CAYLEY H.	PRIVATE	6th BUFFS
CHAMBERLAIN W.C.	SERGEANT	HOME COUNTIES FIELD AMBULANCE
CHAMBERLAIN WILLIAM		6th BUFFS
CHANDLER C.	PRIVATE	2nd BUFFS
CHANDLER CLARENCE		ROYAL ENGINEERS
CHANDLER THOMAS		ROYAL ENGINEERS
CHANDLER W.	BOMBADIER	29th BATT R F A
CLARKE A.	LANCE CORPORAL	SIGNAL CO. R E
CLARKE C.	LANCE CORPORAL	ROYAL ENGINEERS
CLAY HARRY	PRIVATE	7th REG NEW BRUNSWICK RANGERS
COLLYER J B	PRIVATE	BUFFS
COOK W	PRIVATE	2nd BUFFS
COPPINS C.	PRIVATE	6th SECTION A V CORPS
COTTER EDWARD	LEADING SEAMAN	H M S DOON
COTTER MICHEAL	LEADING SEAMAN	H M S BLENHEIM
COX F.	1st CLASS BOY	H M S AGAMEMNON
COX F.	PRIVATE	ARMY SERVICE CORPS
CRAIG NORMAN	LIEUTENANT COMMANDER	R N
CRO A.E.	2nd CLASS SEAMAN	R N
CRO W.E		2nd K C B
CROOM E.	LANCE CORPORAL	4th BATT RIFLE BRIGADE
CROUCHER	STOKER P O	R N
CURRICK L.	PRIVATE	2nd BUFFS
CURTISS CYRIL MICHEAL	PRIVATE	ROYAL WEST KENT REGIMENT
DACK ARTHUR		TORPEDO BOAT 35
DACK C.W.	ARTIFICER	R N R
DACK CHAS		H M S ALBATROSS
DANIELS LEN	A B	H M S OFFSPRAY
DARBY	LANCE CORPORAL	6th BUFFS
DARBY A.E.	LANCE CORPORAL	6th BUFFS
DAVIS	CORPORAL	NO 1 VETINARY HOSPITAL
DAWE H.C.	GUNNER	R F A
DAY PERCY GEORGE	1st CLASS BOY	R N
DEAN I P	PRIVATE	R A M C
DEFREDUS E.	DRIVER	MECHANICAL TRANSPORT A S C
DEFREDUS J.	DRIVER	MECHANICAL TRANSPORT A S C
DENNIS A.	GUNNER	R F A
DENNIS G.	A B	H M S GANGES
DENNIS H.	GUNNER	R F A
DOUST JOHN	PRIVATE	4th BUFFS
DRAKELEY D.H.	PRIVATE	ROYAL SUSSEX REGIMENT
DRAKELEY J.J.	PRIVATE	ROYAL WEST KENT REGIMENT
DRAYSON E.	TROOPER	6th DRAGOON GUARDS
DRAYSON S.J.A.	A B	H M S NATAL
DUNBAR H.F.	A B	H M S VENGEANCE
DUNBAR PAUL	SERGEANT INSTRUCTOR	KINGS OWN LANCASTER REG
EMERY GEORGE	LIEUTENANT	4th ESSEX REGIMENT
EMERY JAMES	CAPTAIN	5th THANET CO 4th BUFFS
EMERY T.S.	LIEUTENANT	CABLE CO. ROYAL ENGINEERS
EMPTAGE C.	PRIVATE	9th LANCERS
EMPTAGE E.	PRIVATE	6th BUFFS
EMPTAGE H.	PRIVATE	6th BUFFS
ENGLAND G.	DRIVER	ARMY SERVICE CORPS
FAGG ALFRED		R F A
FAGG ALFRED		R F A
FAGG HY		H M S MATCHLESS
FASHAM F.	PRIVATE	4th BUFFS
FASHAM N.	PRIVATE	7th BUFFS
FELLS AUBREY		BUFFS
FERRIS C.	DRIVER	ROYAL FIELD ARTILLERY
FOWELLS AUBREY		4th BUFFS
FOWLER T.	DRIVER	MECHANICAL TRANSPORT
FREEMAN FRANK	NAVAL ARTIFICER	DEVONPORT
FRIEND G.M.	CORPORAL	3rd KENT BATTERY R F A
FULLER W.F.	GUNNER	3rd HOME COUNTIES R F A
GARDNER C.	A B	H M S FORMIDABLE
GARDNER G.C.	PRIVATE	2nd BUFFS
GARDNER H.G.	PRIVATE	2nd BUFFS

Name	Rank	Unit
GARDNER S	SIGNALMAN	MALTA
GARDNER W.	PRIVATE	6th BUFFS
GIBBENS S.	PRIVATE	ARMY SERVICE CORPS
GIBBONS JOHN	PRIVATE	LONDON FIELD AMBULANCE R A M C
GIBBY A.A.	GUNNER	AMMINITION COLUMN
GIBBY H.	DRIVER	ROYAL HORSE ARTILLERY
GILBERT BERT		BUFFS
GILBERT F.C.	BOMBADIER	39th ROYAL FIELD ARTILLERY
GILBERT FRED		BUFFS
GILLET HARRY		KENT CYCLISTS
GILLETT	A B	H M S UNDAUNTED
GILLETT W.R.		H M S UNDAUNTED
GILLIS J.		15th HUSSARS
GITTENS	CORPORAL	ROYAL WEST SUSSEX REGIMENT
GODDARD	PRIVATE	NO 10 VETINARY HOSPITAL
GOODEY J. R.	RIFLEMAN	RIFLE BRIGADE
GOSNEY G.	PRIVATE	ROYAL WELSH FUSILERS
GREENWOOD H.	A B	H M S ERIN
GREENWOOD WM	A B	H M S ERIN
GREY	DRIVER	ROYAL FIELD ARTILLERY
GULLICK A.L.	LIEUTENANT	6th BATT BUFFS
GULLICK C.D.	LIEUTENANT	6th BATT BUFFS
GULLICK G.M.	2nd LIEUTENANT	3rd BUFFS
GULLICK L.B.		R N V R
GULLICK T.E.	LIEUTENANT	ARMY SERVICE CORPS
GUTSELL	PRIVATE	4th BUFFS
HAGGARD D.	MIDSHIPMAN	H M S OTWAY
HALE LESLEY		KENT CYCLIST BATTALION
HAMMOND	GUNNER	ROYAL GARRISON ARTILLERY
HAMMOND GEORGE T.		R N
HAMMOND P.E.	GUNNER	C BATT ROYAL HORSE ARTILLERY
HAMMOND PERCY		R H A
HAMMOND THOMAS		R N COASTGUARD
HAMMOND WILLIAM		ROYAL ENGINEERS
HARDING EDWARD	PRIVATE	9th BUFFS
HARRIS G.	A B	H M S DOMINION
HARRIS G.D.	SAPPER	ROYAL ENGINEERS
HARRIS W.T.	A B	H M S DOMINION
HARRISON	PRIVATE	2nd ROYAL SUSSEX REGIMENT
HARRISON A.	PRIVATE	5th BUFFS
HARTY ALFRED		H M S NATAL
HARVEY ARTHUR		BUFFS
HARVEY ARTHUR		3rd BUFFS
HASTINGS F.W.	GUNNER	R A
HATCHETT S.	PRIVATE	4th BUFFS
HAVERKAMP A.	LANCE CORPORAL	ROYAL FIELD ARTILLERY
HEATH SYDNEY		BUFFS
HEGSTON R.	PRIVATE	4th BUFFS
HERSE JOHN		8th QUEENS R W SURREY
HEWETT W	GUNNER	R H A
HEWITT A.	A B	H M S IPHEGINIA
HILL H.	A B	H M S VENGEANCE
HILLER E.G.	PRIVATE	ARMY SERVICE CORPS
HILLER J.	CORPORAL	MILITARY MOUNTED POLICE
HILLER J.C.	CORPORAL	MILITARY MOUNTED POLICE
HILLS ALBERT		WEST KENT REGIMENT
HILLS ALBERT E.	LANCE SERGEANT	2nd ROYAL WEST KENT REGIMENT
HILLS FRANK ERNEST	PRIVATE	3rd BUFFS
HILLS H.W.	CORPORAL	EAST KENT REGIMENT
HINKLEY P.	SAPPER	ROYAL ENGINEERS
HOBDAY A.S.	PRIVATE	ROYAL WEST KENT REGIMENT
HODGES A.	A B	
HODGES E.	PRIVATE	4th BUFFS
HODINOTT H	PRIVATE	BUFFS
HOGSTON GEORGE	GUNNER	ROYAL GARRISON ARTILLERY
HOLLANDS ALF	1st CLASS P O	H M S LORD NELSON
HOLLANDS H.A.	A B	H M S CALLIOPE
HOLLANDS W.E.	STOKER	H M S CORNWALLIS
HOLLANDS WILLIAM		H M S CONRWALLIS
HOLLEY E.	CORPORAL	ARMY SERVICE CORPS
HORNE J.F.	1st CLASS P O	H M S CRESSY
HURLEY G.	PRIVATE	BUFFS
HYMERS F W	DRIVER	3rd KENT BATT R F A (T)
IMPETT A.B.	CORPORAL	BUFFS
INGLETON W.	COOK	H M S ST GEORGE
INGRAM S.W.	LIEUTENANT	6th BUFFS
ISITT C.	TROOPER	EAST KENT YEOMANRY
ISITT C.E.		R A M C
JACKSON P.H.	CORPORAL	6th BUFFS
JACKSON THOMAS		ROYAL ENGINEERS
JAMES	PRIVATE	4th SECTION LABOUR COMPANY
JARMAN ALF	PRIVATE	4th BUFFS

JARMAN C L.		1st BUFFS
JARMAN E.	PRIVATE	2nd BUFFS
JARMAN E.L.	PRIVATE	2nd BATT BUFFS
JARVIS REGINALD		R F A
JENKINS C		R N
JENKINS ERNEST		H M S WEYMOUTH
JENKINS FRANK		H M A S AUSTRALIA
JENKINS JOHN		H M S NATAL
JENKINS NELSON		H M S PETREL
JOHNSON HARRY		R W K
JOHNSON P	PRIVATE	4th WORCESTER REGIMENT
JOOD GEO	P C TEL	H M S PATROL
JORDAN A.E.	SEAMAN	H M S CREASEY
JORDAN E.	PRIVATE	R A M C
JORDAN F.	PRIVATE	4th BUFFS
JORDAN H.	PRIVATE	R A M C
JORDAN S.	PRIVATE	4th BUFFS
JORDAN W.S.	PRIVATE	4th BUFFS
KING H.C.	BOMBADIER	ROYAL FIELD ARTILLERY
KING ROBERT	TROOPER	EAST KENT YEOMANRY
KIRBY C.J.	PRIVATE	1st BUFFS
KIRBY C.J.		1st BATTALLION BUFFS
KNOTT F.H.	PRIVATE	ROYAL WEST KENT REGIMENT
KNOTT H.J.	SAPPER	ROYAL ENGINEERS
LAMBERT E.		WIRELESS T R U
LANGMAN BOYD		R A M C
LARKINS CLAUDE	MIDSHIPMAN	H M S TRIUMPH
LARKINS R.C.	ASST PAYMASTER	H M S MANCO
LASLETT HAROLD		R F A
LASLETT L.H.T.	PRIVATE	4th BUFFS
LAWRENCE BOYCE	PRIVATE	R A M C
LEGGE T.C.	2nd LIEUTENANT	NATIONAL RESERVE
LEIGHTON W.	SERGEANT INSTRUCTOR	ARTISTS RIFLES
LEWIS E.C.R.	PRIVATE	3rd HOME COUNTIES R F A
LEWIS ERIC		KENT CYCLISTS BATTALLION
LEWIS H.	SAPPER	ROYAL ENGINEERS
LEWIS H.	SAPPER	ROYAL ENGINEERS
LEWIS R.W.	ACT CORPORAL	RIFLE BRIGADE
LIGHTFOOT RALPH		R N D
LONG S.T.	PRIVATE	1st BUFFS
LOVE CYRIL		CANADIAN CONTINGENT
LOVE LEONARD		H M S TEMERAIRE
LOVE MARSHALL		R W K R
LOVEGROVE GEORGE WILL	PRIVATE	ROYAL MARINE LIGHT INFANTRY
MACDONOUGH H.	PRIVATE	K R R
MACDONOUGH M	BANDMASTER	K R R
MACDONOUGH WM	SERGEANT	BUFFS
MAHONEY E.	PRIVATE	6th BATTALLION BUFFS
MAITLAND G.H.	P O	H M S LEGION
MANUEL A.J.		NATIONAL RESERVE
MARKWELL T.	PRIVATE	4th BUFFS
MARSH D.M.	SERGEANT	4th BUFFS
MARSH R.	P O	H M S EURYALUS
MARSHALL C.	PRIVATE	3rd BATT COLDSTREAM GUARDS
MARTIN WILLIAM	P O	H M S PENELOPE
MASTERS A.	PRIVATE	1st BUFFS
MAXTED H.	STOKER	H M S HAMPSHIRE
MAXTED W.	SIGNALMAN	H M T B SYREN
MAY F.F.		MESS 10 R N BARRACKS
MAY F.W.	SERGEANT	ROYAL WEST KENT REGIMENT
MAYERS	PRIVATE	1st BUFFS
MAYHILL A.E.	LANCE CORPORAL	9th BUFFS
MCGAVIN F.	SERGEANT	ARMY SERVICE CORPS
MCGAVIN S.	PRIVATE	R A M C
MEASDAY E.	PRIVATE	4th BUFFS
MERCER E.	PRIVATE	1st BUFFS
MERCER G.	CORPORAL	8th SERVICE BATT BUFFS
MERCER JOHN		4th BUFFS
MERRICK R.	ORDINARY SEAMAN	H M S HIBERNIA
MIDDLECOTE THOMAS		1st SOUTH AFRICAN INFANTRY
MIDDLECOTE W.H.	PRIVATE	K C B
MILES	GUNNER	MACHINE MOTOR GUN SECTION
MILLAR R.	TROOPER	EAST KENT YEOMANRY
MILLER A.G.	PRIVATE	6th BUFFS
MILLER EDGAR		R F A
MILLER H.G.	PRIVATE	6th BUFFS
MILLER HERBERT		SOUTH WALES BORDERERS
MILLER J.	PRIVATE	7th BUFFS
MILLER J.	PRIVATE	BUFFS
MILLER JOHN		BUFFS (T)
MILLER RICHARD		R W K
MILLER T.	STOKER	H M S CREASEY

Name	Rank	Unit
MILLER W.J.		H M S AFRICA
MILLS H.A.	PRIVATE	3rd BUFFS
MILLS H.A.	PRIVATE	3rd BUFFS
MILWAY EDWIN H.		R A M C (STAFF)
MOCKETT GORDON	CAPTAIN	ROYAL IRISH RIFLES
MOCKETT WILL SHERWOOD	LIEUTENANT	LONDON BRIGADE ROYAL FIELD ARTILL
MORGAN A.T.	PRIVATE	6th BUFFS
MOSS T.A.	LIEUTENANT	ARMY SERVICE CORPS
MOUNT F.	PRIVATE	5th BUFFS ATT ROYAL WEST KENT REG
MUGGLETON R.	A B	H M S DOMINION
MUGGRIDGE FRED	PRIVATE	4th BUFFS
MUIR J.	PRIVATE	21st LANCERS
MUIR WALLACE	PRIVATE	4th SUSSEX
NASH E.C.	PRIVATE	1st CITY OF LONDON SANITARY CO
NASH F C	LIEUTENANT	9th BUFFS
NASH W.W.E.	SERGEANT	7th BATTALLION BUFFS
NEALE	TROOPER	21st LANCERS
NEALE PERCY		5th BUFFS
NEAME	BOMBADIER	R F A
NEVARD E.C.	CORPORAL	17th SECTION ARMY VETINARY CORPS
NEVILLE ARCHIBALD		ARMY SERVICE CORPS
NEVILLE W.	SERGEANT	ARMY SERVICE CORPS
NORMAN	CORPORAL	6th BUFFS
NOTT M.	LIEUTENANT	ROYAL FLYING CORPS
NUTTING TOM.	PRIVATE	R A M C
NUTTING W.	PRIVATE	6th BUFFS
OAK-RHIND B.H.	GUNNER	ROYAL GARRISON ARTILLERY
OSBORNE G.	PRIVATE	EAST KENT YEOMANRY
OVENDEN C.	A B	H M S CHATHAM
OVENDEN W.	PRIVATE	6th BUFFS
PADBURY E.T.	STOKER	H M S CYNTHIA
PAGE REGINALD	SIGNAL BOY	H M S WALLAROO
PANTONT H G.	PRIVATE	ARMY SERVICE CORPS
PANTONY A.	STOKER	H M S HIBERNIA
PANTONY A.E.	GUNNER	ROYAL GARRISON FORCES S A
PANTONY C.W.	PRIVATE	1st BATT QUEENS ROYAL WEST SURRY
PANTONY F.	RIFLEMAN	3rd BATT KINGS ROYAL RIFLES
PANTONY H.	STOKER P O	H M S PHOENIX
PANTONY LES	1st CLASS BOY	CHATHAM
PANTONY P.	RIFLEMAN	3rd RIFLE BRIGADE
PANTONY R.	TROOPER	EAST KENT YEOMANRY
PANTONY R.J.	PIONEER	KENT SIGNAL CO. R E
PARISH	CORPORAL	SUSSEX REGIMENT
PARISH CHARLES	SERGEANT	KINGS ROYAL RIFLES
PARISH WALTER	PRIVATE	R A M C
PASBURY A.V.	A B	H M S RESTANGE
PEARSON F.H.	PRIVATE	KENT CYCLIST BATTALION
PEMBLE FRED		R F A
PEMBLE WALTER		R F A
PETLEY	PRIVATE	ARMY VETINARY CORPS
PETLEY ALBERT		BUFFS
PETLEY G.H.	PRIVATE	BUFFS
PETLEY W.J.		H M S PANDORA
PETTEY ED	STOKER P O	H M S DOON
PETTIT JACK		4th BUFFS
PETTS H.T..	PRIVATE	2nd BUFFS
PETTS W.	PRIVATE	6th BUFFS
PEYTON	COMMANDER	R N
PHILLIPS J.D.	LIEUTENANT	EAST KENT REGIMENT
PHILPOTT A.	PRIVATE	4th BUFFS
PHILPOTT F.N.	RIFLEMAN	1st RIFLE BRIGADE
PIGGOTT F.E.	STAFF SERGEANT MAJOR	5th BATT AUSTRALIAN FORCE
PITCHER R.C.	PRIVATE	2nd BUFFS
POWELLS WILLIAM		R F A
PRICE G.H.	SERGEANT MAJOR	1st KENT CYCLISTS
PRICE JOHN	SERGEANT	BUFFS
RANCE H.	CORPORAL	R A M C
READER J.	PRIVATE	3rd BUFFS
REDMAN H.V.	SERGEANT	R A M C
RENNOLS JOCK		H M M B PUFFIN
RICHARDSON E.	CORPORAL	3rd HUSSARS
RICHARDSON R.E.	SAPPER	ROYAL ENGINEERS
ROBINSON A.	SERGEANT	INLAND WATER TRANSPORT R E
ROBINSON C.A.	SERGEANT	6th BUFFS
ROBINSON HORACE	PRIVATE	2nd BUFFS
ROBINSON W.N.	PRIVATE	ARMY SERVICE CORPS
ROBINSON W.N.	MECHANICIAN	H M S KING EDWARD VII
ROBSON J.N.	LIEUTENANT	R A M C
ROGERS E.	PRIVATE	R A M C
ROGERS J.S.V.	PRIVATE	ARMY SERVICE CORPS
ROSS I.	MIDSHIPMAN	H M S KENT
SACKETT	DRIVER	MOTOR TRANSPORT CORPS

Name	Rank	Unit
SAMSON G.	PRIVATE	6th BUFFS
SAMSON R.	DRIVER	R F A
SAMSON R.	GUNNER	R F A
SANGSTER A.W.	CAPTAIN	4th BUFFS
SAUNDERS A.G.	SAPPER	ROYAL ENGINEERS
SAUNDERS E.R.	LANCE CORPORAL	8th BATT THE BUFFS
SAUNDERS ERNEST		R W S R
SAUNDERS F.	CORPORAL	NATIONAL RESERVE
SAYER W.	PRIVATE	R A M C
SEAGER THOMAS	LANCE CORPORAL	7th DRAGOON GUARDS
SEERS T.		H M S TERROR
SEERS W.T.		H M S RUSSELL
SERGEANT T.W.		R N
SETTERFIELD A.A.	SERGEANT	ROYAL FIELD ARTILLERY
SETTERFIELD F.W.	PRIVATE	7th BUFFS
SETTERFIELD G.T.	PRIVATE	4th BUFFS
SETTERFIELD J.	STOKER	H M S HOGUE
SHADWELL LANCELOT C.	2nd LIEUTENANT	ARMY SERVICE CORPS
SHAXTED G.	PRIVATE	6th BUFFS
SHELVEY P.W.	PRIVATE	R A M C
SHERRED	SERGEANT	ARMY SERVICE CORPS
SHERSBY H R	STOKER	H M S RUSSELL
SHERSBY H.	A B	H M S DOMINION
SHERSBY S.	PRIVATE	R A M C
SILK S.G.	A B	H M S GANGES
SIMMONS L.	GUNNER	R F A
SKILTON H.J.	RIFLEMAN	1st BATALLION RIFLE BRIGADE
SKINNER HUGH W.	2nd LIEUTENANT	3rd HOME COUNTIES BRIGADE R F A
SKINNER M.N.		2nd BATT KENT CYCLISTS
SMART E.	DRIVER	31st BRIGADE R F A
SMITH C.H.	LANCE CORPORAL	2nd BUFFS
SMITH CHAS	CORPORAL 1st CLASS SCOUT	BUFFS
SMITH H.S.	PRIVATE	2nd BUFFS
SMITH H.S.	CORPORAL	2nd BUFFS
SMITH J.F.G.	LIEUTENANT	5th DURHAM LIGHT INFANTRY
SNOAD H.G.		ROYAL WEST KENT REGIMENT
SNOWDEN HARCOURT JOHN	LIEUTENANT	1st HERTFORDSHIRE RIFLES
SOLE	SAPPER	ROYAL ENGINEERS
SOLLY A.	GUNNER	R F A
SOPER C.H.	PRIVATE	ARMY SERVICE CORPS
SOUTHERN J.	PRIVATE	QUEENS OWN REGIMENT
SPAIN W.T.	DRIVER	2nd SIEGE BATTERY
STANLEY P.H.	PRIVATE	A V C NO 1 HOSPITAL
STEED JAS	GUNNER	R F A
STEED JOHN	GUNNER	R F A
STEVENS E.A.		R A M C
STEWART A.H.	QUARTER MASTER SERGEANT	1st CITY OF LONDON SANITARY ENG
STEWART A.L.		2nd CITY OF LONDON ROUGHRIDERS
STOKES E G.	STOKER PO	H M TORPEDO BOAT 8
STREVENS W.		ROYAL NAVY AIR SERVICE
STRONG ALBERT	A B	H M S ABOUKIR
STUPPLES E.	A B	H M S HAWKE
SULTAN CYRIL		ROYAL ENINEERS SIGNAL SECTION
SUTTON C.E.	PIONEER	NO.3 SEC SIGNAL CO. R E
SUTTON W.L.	PRIVATE	QUEENS ROYAL; WEST SURRY REG
SUTTON W.L.	A B	H M S LAPWING
SWAINE A.	CYCLIST	1st ARMY CYCLIST CORPS
SWAINE S	LANCE CORPORAL	2nd BATTALLION KENT CYCLISTS
TAPPENDEN A.	BUGLER	3rd BUFFS
TAPPENDEN E.	STOKER	H M S KING EDWARD
TAPPLY ARTHUR		R F A
TAYLOR G.L.	BOMBADIER	R F A
TAYLOR STANLEY		1st BUFFS
TEMPLE E.C.	1st CLASS PO	H M S SHANNON
THIRKETTLE HERBERT	PRIVATE	AUSTRALIAN CONTINGENT
THIRKETTLE P.	BOMBADIER	132 nd BATT R F A
THIRKETTLE W	LANCE CORPORAL	A S C
THOMPSON P.	LANCE CORPORAL	6th BUFFS
TOMLIN HARRY	LEADING STOKER	H M S ARETHUSA
TOMLIN WILLIAM	A B	H M S JUNO
TOOP B.W.	PRIVATE	ARMY SERVICE CORPS
TUCKER ERNEST WILLIAM	PRIVATE	7th BATTALLION BUFFS
TUCKER JOHN ARTHUR	BOMBADIER	ROYAL GARRISON ARTILLERY
TURNER F.	STOKER	H M S NELSON
TURNER FRED		R N WIRELESS STATION
TURNER R.H.	PRIVATE	7th BUFFS
VAN DE VEN LESLIE	PRIVATE	15th BATT CIVIL SERVICE RIFLES
WALKER W.	SERGEANT	BEDFORDSHIRE REGIMENT
WALTER BERT	PRIVATE	7th BUFFS
WALTER FRED	PRIVATE	R F A
WARDLE EDWARD		R F A
WARNER RICHARD		BUFFS

Name	Rank	Unit
WARNER WILLIAM		R F A
WARREN L.	PRIVATE	ROYAL FUSILERS
WARREN LES	GUNNER	R F A
WEBB E.	PRIVATE	BUFFS
WELLS A.J.	SAPPER	ROYAL ENGINEERS
WESTCOTT THOMAS E.	1st BOY	H M S INFLEXIBLE
WESTON ALFRED CYRIL	PRIVATE	R A M C
WESTON H.	LIEUTENANT	THE BUFFS
WESTON J.W.	PRIVATE	R A M C
WHITE A.		H M S IMPREGNABLE
WHITE CYRIL E.	3rd OFFICER	H M HIRED TRANSPORT BARON NAPIER
WHITE O DARKIN	CHIEF OFFICER	H M HIRED TRANSPORT ELEPHANTA
WHITE ROY	TROOPER	QUEENS OWN WORCESTERSHIRE HUSSARS
WHITE WILLIAM		BUFFS
WHITEHEAD W.	PRIVATE	1st BUFFS
WHITEING WILLIAM		SOUTH WALES BORDERERS
WHITEING WM	PRIVATE	BUFFS
WICKHAM	SUB LIEUTENANT	4th DRAGOON GUARDS
WICKHAM E.T.	LIEUTENANT	H M S ARGYLE
WICKHAM F.	ST B SURGEON	H M S ALERT
WICKHAM JOHN	PRIVATE	2nd BUFFS
WICKHAM W.H.	PRIVATE	2nd BUFFS
WIGGINGTON C.	1st CLASS STOKER	H M TORPEDO BOAT LAPWING
WIGGINGTON C.H.		H M TORPEDO BOAT 34
WILLIAMS D.	PRIVATE	22nd BATT MIDDLESEX REGIMENT
WILLIAMS MOSTYN	PRIVATE	R A M C
WILLIAMS ROGER	LIEUTENANT	R A M C
WILSON E.	PRIVATE	ARMY SERVICE CORPS
WINSLEY LLOYD	DRIVER	MECHANICAL TRANSPORT A S C
WISH E.C.	CORPORAL	2nd WILTSHIRE REGIMENT
WISH E.J.	A B	R N V R
WOOD A.	A B	ROYAL NAVY
WOOD CHAS	PRIVATE	R A M C
WOOD ERNEST	PRIVATE	1st BATT ROYAL WEST KENT REGIMENT
WOOD GER	SERGEANT	GRENADIER GUARDS
WOODIN	PRIVATE	7th CITY OF LONDON REGIMENT
WOODRUFF	PRIVATE	ARMY VETINARY CORPS
WOODWARD E.	PRIVATE	8th BUFFS
WOODWARD ERNEST	PRIVATE	4th ROYAL WEST KENTS
WOODWARD WM	SERGEANT	1st BUFFS
WOODWARD WM	PRIVATE	GRENADIER GUARDS
WRATTEN	SEAMAN	H M S HAWKE
YEOMAN ALBERT	SIGNALMAN	ROYAL ENGINEERS

BROADSTAIRS & ST PETERS WAR MEMORIALS

During 1919, most of the troops who had survived the Great War were returning home, & like most other towns, memorials to those that didn't survive were actively being thought about. In Broadstairs, the biggest issue was in what form the memorial was to take. As custodians of the town, the Urban District Council took control, but the local churches wished to have a larger input into the subject as it was thought that memorials were more their province than the councils. All necessary money was to come from the townspeople, so the circle of people to be satisfied, like the recently formed ratepayers association, & the Comrades Association had to be taken into account. After protracted arguments the council & the churches agreed to go their own ways on the subject, though the council considered that there were too many memorials being proposed, & the total amount of money being collected was being watered down.

Holy Trinity Church in Broadstairs was very quick off the mark, & discussions as to whether to finish off modifying the church, which was stopped just before 1914, was a suitable purpose for a memorial was discounted. Money came in very fast from the prosperous parishioners of this part of town, & a wayside calvary was commissioned in July 1919. This was installed in the wall of the church facing Albion Street, & was dedicated by the Rev. L. L Edwards on November 11th 1919, one year after the armistice was signed, & was described as "a magnificent tribute to the memory of all Bradstonians who fell for the great cause". The full size figure of Christ was cast in bronze as was the tribute tablets, the wooden cross was originally made in Baltic pine, with the intention of changing it to teak when money allowed.

Meanwhile the town council dithered. By February 1919, a committee of ten under the chairmanship of Dr Brightman was formed, who were given the task of looking for suitable suggestions with appropriate costs & the practicality for each. Amongst those on the list were a Broadstairs cottage hospital, sponsorship for beds or a ward at either of the other Ramsgate's or Margate's cottage hospitals, Almshouses for the poor, an education fund for orphaned boys of servicemen, town baths & a washhouse, the erection of three drinking fountains, a home for disabled servicemen, a town monument, a new motor fire engine, a memorial recreation ground, & the reinstatement of the lifeboat. All were considered to be worthy causes, but the longer the list grew, the longer the arguments became.

HOLY TRINITY WAR MEMORIAL

In May 1919, a sub committee of five was set up under the chairmanship of Dr Raven, Messrs Weigall, Emery, Gullick, & Miss Eveling were also on the committee, whose job was to look into costing. They came up with the following. An 8 bed cottage hospital with the land, buildings & fittings would come to £3,000. An annuity of £10,000 would be required to run it. Almshouses for ten inmates would come to £4,000 for land & buildings, with 10s per week per inmate. A 6 acre recreation ground & pavilion would cost £3,000. Three wayside drinking fountains would cost £500 each. Other suggestions, such as a new fire engine was not considered as it would soon wear out & therefore not appropriate as a permanent memorial. The idea of asking the R.N.L.I. for a lifeboat back again, as the last one had been removed in 1912, was also ruled out, but the local boatmen said that they would petition for one anyway.

The committee reported back to the main body of the council in September, recommending that the memorial recreation ground was the most practical solution. The arguments started all over again. The ratepayers & Comrades club representatives were all for the idea of the memorial recreation ground, others claimed, "a *recreation ground used properly for fetes, music, games & gaiety is the last thing that should be considered as a permanent memorial*". The proposal of a new Government Health Act was considered to overtake any form of hospital memorial, though Councillor Emery said, "*I suggested a cottage hospital for Broadstairs for the 1897 jubilee, & I'll suggest it again. I hope I will never see anything such as government hospitals, & I believe the whole country would be rise up against such a suggestion"*. The idea of a fixed memorial in the form of a statue to the fallen installed in the gardens on the seafront was gathering momentum. Still no one new how much money would be available for a memorial, so the council passed a resolution to collect donations first, & decide what would be appropriate for the money raised. More objections were raised as people would only give money if they thought the memorial would be appropriate to them.

The seasonal entertainers in the town led the way, & impromptu memorial concerts were formed, with £230 being raised in the first month. A concert by the Royal Marines at the bandstand, supported by Miss Margaret Cooper, with the bandstand being decorated with flags & ferns, a large white ensign from the Zebrugge raid, Chinese lanterns & fairy lights, raised £200 in one evening alone.

Running parallel with idea of a permanent memorial was the War Office Trophy Commission. The war office was offering captured war trophies for display or for incorporating into war memorials to town councils. Not wanting to miss out Broadstairs Council like Ramsgate applied. What was offered was considered an insult to the two towns, particularly after the onslaught that Ramsgate had received. Each town was offered a damaged German machine gun & damaged ammunition box. After Folkestone had been promised a German Gotha Bomber for display, Broadstairs council commented on their offering as "*a great disappointment. If that is all we are going to get, we are not going to get very much. It is the same all along for Thanet, we should at least have a howitzer, or at least something worth looking at*". Ramsgate's machine gun was actually sent, & the railway station master wanted it off his premises, as soon as possible. The councillor's suggestion was to either send it for scrap, or mount it on the green in Boundary Road, "*for the kiddies to play with*". Broadstairs hung out for a small German aeroplane but finally got a captured 4.9 mm German howitzer, which was delivered to the railway station, & with much of a struggle was removed to the council's yard behind Crampton's water tower for a repaint in November 1919, where it stayed for the next four years. A final decision was made as to where to put it. After more months of discussion, it was decided to put it in the park next to Pierremont Hall, "*where we can keep an eye on it*", being finally installed in December 1923.

By the end of the year, (1919), a little over £500 had been raised for the war memorial, & a general air of disgust from those who had fought, & relatives of those who had fallen were directed at the council. The impetus was waning as time passed, & like other projects in the council's hands it was feared that nothing would ever happen. A decision was made as to what type of memorial was wanted, but the stumbling block was where to put it. In 1921 a decision was finally made & the council approached Dan Mason, the owner of Pierremont Park & the Hall, whether it could be sited in the park facing the High Street, where a half circle of 30 feet would be required. Though the council had leased the Hall, with the right to buy the previous year from Dan Mason, he turned the council suggestion down, so another site on council owned land was sought. A final, final, decision was then made & a suitable site at the bottom of Westcliffe Road, to the south of the Grand Hotel, on the Western Esplanade, with a view over the sea to France, where most of the men had died was found to be most suitable. Councillor Ridgeway said, "*There has been a great deal of talk backwards & forwards on the matter, but hoped there would now be peace*". He thought it a most unfortunate thing that with regard to such a question as the war memorial there should be anything like antagonistic feeling, recrimination or squabbling, (hear-hear), & he hoped the town would accept the recommendation of the committee in the manner of the men to whose memory the memorial was to be erected. All the council agreed & Mr Courtenay Pollock, R.B.A, R.B.S, R.W.E.A., was invited in as designing consultant. As only £500 had so far been raised, Mr Pollock suggested having some marble tablets engraved & mounted in a suitable wall, somewhere, an idea that fell on deaf ears within the council. A monument in the form of a cross is what was wanted, & that is what they were going to get. On inspecting the proposed site on the cliff top, Mr Pollock turned down the location as being totally unsuitable, as with the town surveyor, he didn't think the cliff would take such a weight of the structure & it's foundations, so it was back to the drawing board, (& Dan Mason).

Mr Stockley, a member of the War Memorial Committee, personally set about raising another £400 for the memorial fund in the summer of 1921. By March 1922, there was £906 in the coffers & serious discussions as to the design took place with Courteney Pollock. A cross 18 feet high with a crusader's sword on one side, elevated by two small steps was finally agreed upon. Marble or Portland stone was the next problem, but owing to the high cost of marble, Portland stone was soon decided upon, with a final cost of £1,000 settled on.

Dan Mason was then approached again as to the setting within the grounds, but he wouldn't relent. His argument was that as the council had only leased the Hall & grounds from him, & as a Labour Government could come in at any time, & stop the council buying the Hall, he would be left with an expensive residence, & a public monument within private grounds, which would be totally unacceptable to him, & the town's people of Broadstairs. Either they buy the Hall & grounds, or put the memorial elsewhere. The council didn't have the £5,500 to buy the Hall at this time, so it was stalemate.

In April 1922, four prominent Broadstairs people came forward, formed a syndicate, & purchased the Hall & grounds from Dan Mason for the £5,500 required. These were Cllr Dr Frank Brightman, Cllr H Bing, Major H.T. Gulliver, & Mrs Nook. Very strict conditions were put in as to they could only resell to the council, at the same price they paid for it, & within a certain time. They tried to claim the expenses through the war memorial committee, but it fell on deaf ears.

In May 1922 a site meeting was held by the Council of possible locations within the park. As reported by a local resident to the local paper, *"it was a most impressive sight. The Broadstairs Council & members of the War Memorial Committee, assembled together under the canopies of heaven. After a few minutes discussion Cllr Forde, addressed the assembly with a strong flavour of magisterial solemnity, a really fine piece of oratory. Bare headed he stood, like Ajax defying the lightening in the good days of old. And no reporters were present, What copy had been there"*. A site at the entrance gates, open to the public view was finally decided, & alterations to the entrance walls carried out.

BROADSTAIRS WAR MEMORIAL.

So after five years of wrangling, the site, & the design, & the appropriate money were all finally together. Out if it Broadstairs had gained Pierremont Hall, the park, & the bowling greens, probably years earlier than it would have done.

Broadstairs finally got its war memorial which was dedicated on June 16th 1923 by archdeacon the venerable L.J.White-Thompson.

In August 1923, Mrs Bertha Wood, Broadstairs first lady Councillor, when asked for her comments stated, *"I'm afraid I have little respect for municipal enterprise. You lose; you're bound to lose every time. I have carried out a years fight over the memorial, practically single handed. They wanted to stick it on the cliffs near Dumpton, a place where nobody goes apart from 3 months of the year. I wanted it outside the council offices where everyone could see it. There was some difficulty because we didn't own it, (Pierremont Hall), only on a lease. Well then, says I, lets buy it, we shall have to sooner or later. I was outvoted 10 to 1, Alright I said, If you hide it alongside Dumpton Gap, I'll go along & blow it up with a bomb, I'll swear I will. Then there will be a scandal. It's now outside the council offices, as you see. The fight nearly finished me off. I nearly walked out of the council & never go back. But I lost my son in the war. I saw it through"*.

112

St Peters also had problems raising money, & a decision was made to buy the derelict "Orlebar House" in the High Street, & convert it into a Parish Institute. This cost the St Peters war memorial committee £750, & it was soon realised that there would not be enough money to convert the building into an institute so it was demolished. A temporary structure was purchased from Richborough Port, which was provided by the Y,M.C.A. as a cinema for the troops at Stonar. This was 100 feet by 80 feet, & was erected on the "Orlebar" site in the summer of 1921. Arguments followed in St Peters, as they did in Broadstairs. A permanent memorial, preferably within the church grounds is what most of the parishioners wanted, but the need for a parish hall was also felt as being of equal importance. It was decided to treat the two projects as separate issues, & the money spent on the "Orlebar" site would stand, but no more money would come out of the War Memorial Fund. It took till October 11th 1922, before the parish hall was fully erected & opened by the Revs Mathews & Sheppard. At the opening address, the Rev Mathews, said he hoped that the temporary building that they were now all in, would soon be replaced by a more permanent structure. The foundations installed had been constructed to take the new building when it was required. He looked forward to the near future when bricks & mortar would take over from the wood, & the second story was completed. The hut was discovered at Stonar & was being battered to pieces. On hearing of this it was inspected & purchased all within the day. On inspecting it on it's arrival in the village he wondered whether the villagers would consider themselves as having been "had". On the financial side, he said, the site had cost £210, & the legal costs £4 18s. The cost of the hut & carriage was £184 5s & the building contract £987, making the total of £1,438. To make the hut free from debt they would have to find another £689 which would be the first task of the committee. The vicar then went on to thank Misses Ward & Osmond for the £120 that they had raised to purchase 450 chairs. The acceptance of the donated piano was also mentioned.

Cllr H Bing, never one to miss an opportunity, as also at the opening ceremony was Alderman Larkin of Ramsgate, whose company had erected the building, told of an earlier discussion that he'd had with the Rev Sheppard about a common dream The County borough of Thanet, where all the island would be united. Hopefully this newly opened hall could be the meeting place for that council. He was quite convinced that the good people of Broadstairs & St Peters possessed the energy & capabilities of leading the rest of Thanet, & therefore Broadstairs & St Peters should become the ruling power of the rest of Thanet. Alderman Larkin replied, *"all know of my views on a united Thanet. If it ever comes to pass, & that won't be yet, then I shall only be to happy to see St Peters at the heart of it. After all Broadstairs & St Peters had set an example to the rest of Thanet in the movement of economic expansion, which other towns could learn from"*.

By July 1922, the St Peters war memorial contract had been placed in the hands of Mr W Overton, a Broadstairs stonemason, who immediately started work. The memorial was to cost £359, of which £270 had already been raised. The cross & plinth were to be made first & the memorial plaques would have to come later when money allowed. A wall in front of the entrance of the church had to be removed, & the entrance to the churchyard enlarged.

The war memorial was built & was unveiled & dedicated by Bishop of Dover 17th June 1925.

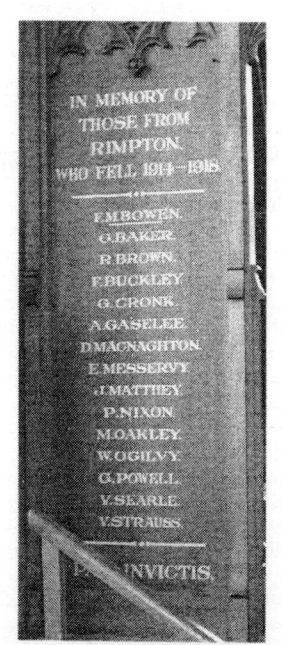

St Andrews, Reading Street. Roll of Honour WW1

IN MEMORY OF THOSE FROM RIMPTON. WHO FELL 1914-1918

F.M.BOWEN.
G.BAKER.
R.BROWN.
F.BUCKLEY.
G.CRONK.
A.GASELEE.
D.MACNAGHTON.
E.MESSERVY.
J.MATTHEY.
P.NIXON.
M.OAKLEY.
W.OGILVY.
G.POWELL.
V.SEARLE.
V.STRAUSS.

INVICTIS.

IN MEMORY OF THOSE FROM THIS VILLAGE AND DISTRICT. WHO FELL 1914-1918.

H.AUSTEN.
W.BAKER.
F.A.BROWN.
A.H.FAGG.
W.GARDNER.
J.GOODEY.
G.W.GOSNEY.
E.HARDING.
F.J.HORN.
R.W.LEWIS.
A.MASTERS.
A.J.MILLER.
J.T.MILLER.
L.A.MILLER.
T.J.MILLER.
J.MURPHY.
F.S.PRETT.
B.WATLER.
S.J.WATLER.
E.WOOD.

THEIR NAME LIVETH

Holy Trinity Dedication Boards to those who fell

GEORGE WILLIAM APPLETON
HORACE EDWIN BOWYER
ROBERT BRENCHLEY
LESLIE BRISLEY
JOB BUNCE
GEORGE BUTCHER
EDWARD JOHN CROOM
HERBERT GILBERT
ROBERT SIDNEY GOODBURN
HUBERT ARTHUR GOODWIN
JOHN ALEXANDER GRANGER
HENRY JOHN HAMMOND
ROBERT HARTY
JOHN HESSE
HERBERT WALTER HILLS

ALFRED HOEDAY
FREDERICK WILLIAM HYMERS
ALBERT JARMAN
JOHN HENRY KNOTT
PERCY JAMES NASH
ALBERT STEPHEN NASH
CHARLES PANTONY
PERCY WILLIAM PANTONY
JOHN ALGERNON WYNYARD PEYTON
MONTAGUE FRANK PEYTON
ROBERT CHARLES PITCHER
JAMES HENRY READER
CYRIL SUTTON
FRANK WALES
FRANK WALSH

ROLL OF HONOUR 1914 — 1918.

G.W.APPLETON.	2ND.OFFR	J.L CASTLE.	DR	G.W.COSNEY.	PTE.
L.W.ARNOLD.	LC.CPL	W.CHAPPELL.	PTE	J.A.GRANGER.	
H.AUSTEN.	SPR	W.M.CHURCHILL.	MAJOR	J.B.GREEN.	LC.SGT.
T.C.B.AUSTEN.	BOY TEL	P.J.CLARK.	SGT	R.G.GREENSTREET.	PTE.
W.BAKER	PTE	S.H.CLEWER.	GR	H.J.GREENWOOD.	P.O.
F.F.BEAN.	STOKER	H.R.CRAYFORD.	PTE	J.H.GREENWOOD.	LC.CPL.
J.H.BING.	GR	E.J.CROOM.	LC.CPL	A.L.GULLICK.	LIEUT.
A.T.BISHOP.	PTE	A.L.DENMEE.	PTE	H.J.HAMMOND.	SGT.
W.C.BISHOP.		W.F.DENMEE.		J.M.HANCOCK.	2ND.LIEUT.
S.H.BLIGHT.		W.A.DIXON.2ND.LIEUT.M.M		E.HARDING.	LC.CPL.
P.L.BLOY.		L.R.C.DOUGLAS-HAMILTON		A.E.HARRIS.	PTE.
P.J.BONES.	LC.CPL		MAJOR	L.A.HARRISON.	SGT.
E.J.BOWLES.	PTE	S.J.A.DRAYSON.ORD.SMN		R.HARRISON.	PTE.
H.E.BOWYER.	DR	A.H.EDIS.	PTE	R.H.HARTY.	GR.
J.E.BRENCHLEY.	PTE	W.O.EDIS.	LIEUT	J.V.HESSE	CPL.
R.H.BRENCHLEY.	P.O	C.E.EMPTACE.	TPR	W.T.HEWETT.	A.B.
W.BRENCHLEY.	GR	A.H.FAGG.	PTE	H.J.HILLER.	SPR.
L.C.BRISLEY.	CPL	M.S.FRAYLING.2ND.LIEUT		H.J.HILLS.	LDG.SMN.
E.C.BRITTON.	PTE	W.E.GARDNER.	PTE	H.W.HILLS.	SGT. D.C.M.
H.J.BROCKMAN.	CPL	L.N.GARSTIN.	LC.CPL	A.S.HOBDAY.	PTE.
F.A.BROWN.	PTE	D.A.C.GIFFORD.	PTE	W.S.HOGBEN.	
L.BROWNE.	CAPT	H.E.GILBERT.		W.A.HOLLIDAY.	
P.H.BUDDS.	LIEUT	S.W.GOATHAM.		J.F.HORN.	P.O
J.BUNGE.	PTE	G.S.GOODBOURN.		F.W.HYMERS.	TRPTR.
A.M.BURNS.		R.S.GOODBURN.		C.E.ISITT.	PTE.
G.J.BUTCHER.		J.J.GOODEY	RFLMN	G.H.JAMES.	
F.H.CASTLE.		W.J.GORHAM.	PTE	A.JARMAN	

S.S.JARMAN.	PTE	J.MURPHY.	P.O	H.J.SNOWDEN.	LIEUT.
J.A.W.JENKINS.	S.B.S	A.S.NASH.	PTE	W.H.SPICE.	PTE.
F.KEMP.	PTE	P.J.NASH.		H.J.SPRINGETT.	CPL.
H.G.P.KENNETT.		A.B.NEALE.		N.H.STOCKDALE.	LIEUT.
C.J.KIRBY.		P.J.NEALE.	TPR	F.C.STOKES.	PTE.
C.J.T.KNIGHT.		CROIX DE GUERRE		A.V.STRONG.	A.B.
J.H.KNOTT.		M.NOOTT.	2ND.LIEUT	C.E.J.SUTTON.	PR.
R.W.LEWIS.	CPL	C.W.PANTONY.	PTE	W.SUTTON.	A.B.
B.P.LINDSAY.	PTE	P.W.PANTONY.	CPL	F.SWAIN.	FARR.SGT.
E.A.C.LLOYD.	LIEUT	J.D.PHILIPS.	LIEUT	M.TANNENBAUM.	PTE.
A.J.MANUEL.	PTE	F.N.PHILPOTT.	RFLMN	E.W.TREVOR.	CAPT.C.F
S.C.S.MARSH.		F.E.PIGGOTT.S.SGT.MAJ		F.A.URRY.	PTE.
A.A.MASTERS.		A.J.PILBEAM.	PTE	L.B.VAN-DE-VEN.	CPL
H.A.V.MATTHEWS.	MAJ.MC	G.W.PILBEAM.LC.BOMBR		W.A.VASSEY.	PTE.
H.MAXTED.	STOKER	R.C.PITCHER.	PTE	F.WALES.	PR.
S.G.McGAVIN.	PTE	F.S.PRETT.		F.J.H.WALSH.	PTE
A.V.MEASDAY.	RFLMN	W.PRICE.		B.H.WATLER.	
A.J.MILLER.	PTE	J.H.READER.		S.J.WATLER	
H.G.MILLER.	SGT	H.REEVES.		H.G.WHITE.	AIR MECH.
J.T.MILLER.	LC.CPL	G.B.SAUNDER.2ND.LIEUT		N.J L.WICKHAM.	CAPT.
L.A.MILLER.	PTE	W.SCOTT.	GR	S.J.WICKHAM.	PTE.
T.J.MILLER.	STOKER	C.A.SETTERFIELD.	STOKER	J.C.WIGGINGTON.	P.O.
L.J.MOON.	LIEUT	G.W.T.SHAXTED.	PTE	C.E.WISH	LC.SGT.
W.E.MOORE.	A.B	K.SHELTON.	CAPT	E.WOOD.	PTE.
R.F.MORTON.	LC.CPL	W.J.SHEPERDON.	PTE	L.J.WOOD.	2ND.LIEUT.
C.MUGGLETON.	LDG.SMN	T.SIMPSON.		E.WOODRUFF.	PTE.
R.S.MUGGLETON.		E.A.F.SMITH.			

Pierremont Roll of Honour WW1

St Peters Roll of Honour

1914 S.H. BLIGHT	Private	J.E. WOOD	Lance Sergeant
R.H. BRENCHLEY	1st Class P.O.	1916 H. AUSTEN	Private
J.J. GOODEY	Rifleman	F.F. BEAN	Stoker
J.F. HORN	1st Class P.O.	J.H. BING	Gunner
F. KEMP	Private	E.J. BOWLES	Private
T.J. MILLER	1st Class P.O.	H. BOWYER	Drummer
A.A. MASTERS	Private	F.A. BROWN	Private
M. NOOTT	2nd Lieutenant	J. BUNCE	Private
C.A. SETTERFIELD	1st Class Stoker	F.H. CASTLE	Private
1915 J.E. BRENCHLEY	Private	LR.CD.OUGLAS-HAMILTON	Major
E.J. CROOM	Lance-Corporal	M.S. FRAYLING	2nd Lieutenant
W.E. GARDNER	Private	G.T. HAMMOND	A.B.
A.L. GULLICK	Lieutenant	E.E. HARDING	Lance-Corporal
R. HARRISON	Private	A.S. HOBDAY	Private
H.J. HILLS	Leading Seaman	F.W. HYMERS	Trumpeter
R.W. LEWIS	Corporal	S.S. JARMAM	Private
A.J. MILLER	Private	A.J. MANUEL	Private
F.N. PHILPOTT	Rifleman	S. MARSH	Private
F.E. PIGGOTT	Staff Sgt Major	H. MAXTED	Stoker
G.W.T. SHAXTED	Private	L.J. MOON	Lieutenant
T. SIMPSON	Private	A.J. PILBEAM	Private
H.J. SNOWDEN	Lieutenant	N.H. STOCKDALE	Lieutenant
A.G. SOLLY	Private	Rev. E.W. TREVOR	Chaplain
C. WISH	Lance-Sergeant		

S.J. WATLER	Private	P.J. NASH	Private	J.V. HESSE	Acting Corporal
N.J.L. WICKHAM	Captain	W. PRICE	Private	W.T. HEWETT	A.B.
1917 T.C.B. AUSTEN	Telegraphist	G.B. SAUNDER	2nd Lieutenant	W.A. HOLLIDAY	Private
W. BAKER	Private	E.A.F. SMITH	Private	H.G.P. KENNETT	Private
E.C. BRITTON	Private	W.H. SPICE	Private	M.A.V. MATTHEWS	M.C. Major
G.J. BUTCHER	Private	F.A. URRY	Private	H.G. MILLER	Sergeant
H.R. CRAYFORD	Private	W.A. VASSEY	Private	C. MUGGLETON	Leading Seaman
A.L. DENMEE	Private	B.H. WATLER	Private	J. MURPHY	1st Class P.O.
W.F. DENMEE	Private	H.G. WHITE	2nd Air Mechanic	A.B. NEALE	Private
C.E. EMPTAGE	Private	J.C. WIGGINTON	Stoker 1st Class P.O.	P.J. NEALE	Private
A.H. FAGG	Private	A. WRIGHT	Private	A.S. NASH	Private
S.W. GOATHAM	Private	1918 G.W. APPLETON	2nd Officer R.N.	G.W. PILBEAM	Bombardier
J.A. GRANGER	Private	H.J. BROCKMAN	Corporal	F.S. PRETT	Private
J.B. GREEN	Lance-Sergeant	J.L. CASTLE	Driver	W.J. SHEPERDON	Private
R.G. GREENSTREET	Private	W. CHAPPELL	Private	H.J. SPRINGETT	Corporal
H.J. HILLER	Sapper	S.H. CLEWER	Gunner	F.C. STOKES	Private
W.S. HOGBEN	Private	W.M. CHURCHILL	Major	W. SUTTON	A.B.
G.H. JAMES	Private	D.A. GIFFORD	Private	S.J. WICKHAM	Private
C.J.T. KNIGHT	Private	R.S. GOODBURN	Private	E. WOODRUFF	Private
E.A.C. LLOYD	Lieutenant	H.J. GREENWOOD	1st Class P.O. T.1.	1919 W. BRENCHLEY	Gunner
S.G. McGAVIN	Private	J.H. GREENWOOD	Lance-Corporal	G.W. GOSNEY	Private
J.T. MILLER	Lance-Corporal	H.J. HAMMOND	Sergeant	A.V. MEASDAY	Private
L.A. MILLER	Private	L.A. HARRISON	Sergeant	W.E. MOORE	A.B.
R. MUGGLETON	A.B.			1920 M. NNENBAUM	Private

St Peters Roll of Honour

The Memorial Recreation Ground

In 1919, Daniel Mason, who owned Pierremont Hall, purchased 8 acres of land by the station which he was going to use as an outside extension to his Pierremont Social Club. This was going to be laid out with a pavilion, football pitches & a cricket pitch. He was so disgusted with internal wranglings of the council on the issue of the war memorial, that he gifted this land to the town as The Memorial Recreation Ground in 1921 as his part of the memorial fund. Even this was accepted slowly by the council as Dan had laid certain stipulations upon it's use. The primary use of the land was to be for the local war veterans in their leisure hours. Visitors & children were to come last. The council's problem was that this would not only require policing, but it meant that the recreation ground would be little used during the weekdays. Dan relented & had a dedicated children's area roped off, & visitors would only be allowed to use it if it wasn't already being used. The other stipulation was that there was to be no pomp or major opening ceremony, which the council readily agreed to. The gates were opened in November 1921, & complaints immediately rolled in from the religious elements of the town regarding ball games, whether organised or not, being played on a Sunday. Councillor Forde's immediate response to this objection was, " *that it did young people just as much good to play games on a Sunday, as it did to attend Sunday schools & similar places. The council were not "killjoys", & providing proper supervision was in place, then no objection would come from the council direction*". Needless to say, you can imagine what the local guardians of Sundays thought of that.

The Memorial Recreation Ground 1922

THE BROADSTAIRS & ST PETERS MAIL

The *Broadstairs & St Peters Mail* was first published on 27th February 1903, under the ownership of the *East Kent Times* a Ramsgate publication. The first office was at No 1 John Street, moving to No 13 The Broadway in 1910, where the newspaper was compiled & published. The title was selected as a tribute to Lord Northcliffe, the owner of the *Daily Mail*, who lived at Elmwood in Reading Street.

Amos Hickmore was the editor until he volunteered to serve his country, loosing his life on the battlefields of France, on the 11th November 1916, at the age of 40.

Stanley Smith took over the editorship after returning injured from the war. He was ably assisted by chief reporter George Reed of St Mildreds Avenue, Broadstairs. Distributed on a Wednesday, the *Broadstairs & St Peters Mail* folded in 1979.

I would like to acknowledge the assistance of Bob Bradley & Terry Meech of The Margate Museum for access to their material, & to Barrie Wootton & Danny Day for their persuasive powers to get this book published.

ADVERTISEMENT :

Michaels Bookshop, 72 King Street, Ramsgate, Kent CT11 8NY
Open Monday-Saturday – 9.30 to 5.30
Closed all day Thursday

Postage to a UK address is free for our own publications.
We charge postage at cost to other countries and are happy to send books to anywhere in the world.

ORDERING ON THE INTERNET   ORDERING BY PHONE
Our website is MichaelsBookshop.com   (01843)589500

You can telephone us between 10am and 5pm Monday - Saturday but not Thursday with your Master card or Visa number You can also leave your Master card or Visa information on our answer phone, if you do please send a confirmatory email including shipping address.

ORDERING BY POST
Payment by cheque UK bank. Cheques payable to Michaels Bookshop

An apology for more than 70 publications (so far) relating to the Southeastern most part of England, a list of them is at the back of this book.
Here in Ramsgate we suffered from a maniacal bibloclast. During 2004 an arson attack on our Carnegie library left it a burnt out shell our large and comprehensive collection of local history books destroyed. Unpublished manuscripts and original works of art that had been donated to the library over the years were lost forever. As the bookseller in the town and a minor collector of local books I felt that I ought to do something, one feels impotent in the face of such destruction.
At the end of 2004 I decided that I would try to make some of the books that one would expect to find in a local history collection available at an affordable price. I also decided that I would try and intercept documents of local significance before they were donated to archives and produce a sufficient number of copies of them to protect them from permanent extinction and that these would also have to be produced at an affordable price to ensure that there were enough copies in different places.
To use a commercial printer and have the sort of quantities of each book produced to make them an affordable price would have meant investing thousands of pounds per book, you can imagine that with over 70 books in print so fa